Sidney C. Sufrin

ETHICS, MARKETS AND POLICY
The Structure of Market Ethics

Studentlitteratur
Chartwell-Bratt

All rights reserved. No part of this publication may be reproduced or transmitted in any form or by any means, electronic or mechanical, including photocopy, recording, or any information storage and retrieval system, without prior permission in writing from the publisher.

Chartwell-Bratt Ltd Bickley, Bromely, United Kingdom
ISBN 0-86238-202-5 Chartwell-Bratt

ISBN 91-44-28971-5
© Sidney C. Sufrin and Studentlitteratur 1989
Printed in Sweden
Studentlitteratur, Lund

Tryckning: 1 2 3 4 5 6 7 8 9 10 | 1993 92 91 90 89

This work is dedicated to the Business Faculty and graduate students of the University of Lund where my wife and I spent such happy hours.

Sidney C. Sufrin

1/2 A Decalogue
Ex Market Ethics

Everyone with some social power has a shot at being ethical in the market context. Business people, especially managers and executives, have a band of discretion which is defined only by the successful use of that discretion. Trade union officials are included in this market oriented classification. Public administrators and legislators, in other words bureaucrats and politicians from the local level to the Halls of Congress and the White House itself, as well as public and private lawyers and judges at all levels, are part of the vast array of people who can and do control aspects of public policy over and above what the words of law might say. The private ethics of each, and each one's perception of the social ethic, nudge, push or shove the rules of society to some degree, great or small.

Self-interest is too blanket a concept to be of much use in evaluating or defining private or public behavior. It is not hard to make a persuasive definition which would include in self interest every and any conceivable freely willed act. Altruistic and ethical behavior can easily be included under the tent of self interest if we define the tent broadly enough. Help for the weak and downtrodden can be interpreted as an avoidance of a guilt gambit. Bravery in battle or in politics can easily be seen as a way to attract attention, even if at a great personal cost. This approach may be classified as cynical or realistic, not that the two words are synonyms. The realist would argue that self interest is very complex and often a hidden motive. The cynic, putting a different emphasis on words, would argue that self interest is very complex and often a hidden motive.

Our experience leads us to neither a cynical nor crudely realistic position. People do sometimes undertake actions which are designed to do good with a minimum of self interest being involved.

Below are a few rules and obervations which might be useful to movers and shakers:

1 Ethical actions are the most noble and valuable manifestations of humankind. Do not expect ethical actions to be costless either in time, money or effort.

2. Do not expect ethical actions to have a payoff for you, other than some vaguely defined sense of self satisfaction. Casting bread on the waters is a way to feed fish, not a way to achieve a fish fry. Ethics which pays off, usually isn't ethical, it is operational.
3. When you deviate from rules and laws becuase you feel it is right to do so, make sure that you or your friends are not the major, nor even the major minor, beneficiaries of the deviation. If you or yours benefit, the action may not be ethical at all, but may merely be clever or selfish.
4. Economists divide their world into short run and long run, and micro and macro. This is a good quartering of the market world. Try to think through the implications of your planned, uncoerced attempts at goodness and ethics in the light of the quadrant. Who may be helped and who hurt by your actions and over what period? Reflex ethics is for the birds, not for people.
5. Regardless of your calling and place in the social scheme of things, the power to do good is a sinful, malethical authority if you believe you can, or actually can seriously influence the lives of others without regard to the restraints and constraints, and checks and balances which human history has so painfully constructed. That power may corrupt is an axiom which holds for all time. A tiny bit of corruption, limited to a feeling of satisfaction, is about all most people can stand and not be obnoxious.

Table of Contents

Preface 11

Chapter I   Ethics, Markets and Politics   13
1   Choice is the Basis   13
2   Money is the Nub   15
3   Constancy – Thy Name is Not Society   15
4   Reason vs. Logic   21
5   The Whole is not the Sum of the Parts   23
6   Market Ethics and Ethics in the Market   27

Part I   35

Chapter II   Are Justice, Fairness and Ethics Real?   37
1   Perceptions and Conceptions   37
2   Some Definitions   39
3   The Use of Ethics   41
4   Ethics of the Market   45
5   Order and Change   47
6   The Perception of Market Ethics   49
7   Inefficiencies as Implicit   52

Chapter III   A Canon of Ethics   54
1   Complexity of Market Ethics   54
2   Morality is Personal   55
3   Reasonable Behavior and Automatic Restraints   58
4   Self Interest is a Reason   60
5   Rote Behavior and Tension   62
6   The Uniqueness of the Ethical Act   63
7   Responsibility is Persistent   66
8   Ethical Acts as Deviant   72

Chapter IV   The Market Ethic and Relevance   74
1 Legitimation   74
2 Management   77
3 The Perception of Ethical Behavior   79
4 Ethics is Like Poetry   82
5 The Imposed Ethic – The Tension of Moral Imperalism   83
6 The Good and Bad of it All   85
7 The Law is Not an Ethic   90

Chapter V   Ethics – Politics – Practicality   93
1 Ideology as Values in Action   93
2 Social Ontology   94
3 Market Ontology   97
4 Ethical Ontology   98
5 Market Efficiency for What?   100
6 Legitimization as Rationalization   104
7 Conclusion   108

Part II   111

Chapter VI   Market Ethics as Market Failure   113
1 Why Theory? Why Ethics?   113
2 Means and Ends   116
3 Market Ethics, Justice and Fairness   119
4 Regulation as an Old Dodge   121

Chapter VII   Law and Economics as Legitimators   124
1 Reality as Assumption   124
2 Two Analytic Tools   126
3 The Legitimation Process   132
4 The Rates of Change   135
5 Criticism and Legitimation   136

Chapter VIII   Professionalism and Business Ethics   143
1 Profession as an Idea   143
2 Business as a Calling, Not as a Profession   145
3 From Ethic to Rule   147

Chapter IX   The Jurisprudence of Markets and Business   150
1 The Setting   150
2 Means and Ends   155
3 Planning of Means and Ends   157

   4 Means and Ends As Conjectures 160
   5 Heterogenity as a Norm 160
   6 The Modern Spirit 161
   7 Ideals 166
   8 The Private and The Social Ethic 167
   9 The Complexity of Interests 170
 10 The Logic of Policy 171

Suggested Readings 174

Index 176

Preface

This study was originally prepared for graduate school and business seminars held at the University of Lund in Sweden during the Spring of 1984. The invitation extended by Professor Gosta Wijk forced me to rethink what I had written and taught about business ethics over the past 5 or 8 years. I have added to the Lund lectures to round out the argument.

I believe the study makes up a coherent analysis of what I now call Market Ethics. To tie ethics to business, is I believe to restrict the discussion to too small a unit. Ethics is a social phenomenon. I am content to grant that my unit, the market, is not the whole gamut of experience. The market is only the process of supply equating to demand, or bids to price.

As I progressed in my thinking I concluded that the role of ethics was not so large as the current litertaure on business ethics suggests. Indeed I now believe that ethical decisions are rare, although often important. The market has its own internal corrections for justice and fairness. Ethics the corrective is, generally speaking, outside the market, at least as I define the moral concept. I guess that I tend to rely more on law and convention than on less organized ways to gain socially and privately approved ends.

When I was much younger I was attracted to the work of George Bernard Shaw and Anatole France, both moralists of sorts. The former in his plays and their long prefaces laid down some general rules. Among the first was that people are unreflective and not motivated sufficiently by ideals of good as Shaw saw such ideals. A second general rule is that Shaw had, by luck or because of his superior insight, managed to capture the content of ethics. While he never out and out told us what the secret was, his characters managed to convey, without much argument among Shaw enthusiasts, what was right and wrong in some contexts. Shaw's genius however was so great that each of us believed himself or herself able to generalize the particulars. This was Shaw's genius, but the genius of a playwright – a moral tactician, not of a moral strategist. The strategic moralist would have written out the categorical imperatives.

Anatole France, on the other hand treated issues of ethics more lightly. For him there were few if any absolutes. To be sure people were funny,

11

silly even comically tragic. Morality was of a time and place, often of a time and place so far from our experience, real or vicarious, that the whole exercise had a dreamlike or perhaps unrealizable ambience.

Shaw is closer to my own belief that life is real and earnest, and not an easy process. But this Puritanical, or possibly egocentric attitude tried to capture the total spirit of morality. That he knew what was good and bad for all and for each is disturbing and frustrating. His attempts to write on economic justice, for example are not noteworthy.

France is of another world. He has no absolutes, he is engaging and even whimsical. But he tells us little of what to do and still be moral. He, in effect, laughs, shrugs his shoulders and says "That's your problem".

Well, it is our problem, but it is not a problem which has but one answer. This I have tried to say in this little work.

My thanks are due to students who are now my colleagues for their help, especially Robin Derry, Richard Molz, John Keller and James Wilson. They have all contributed to the development of the ideas of this work. My colleagues Professors George Odiorne, Joseph Litterer, Pieter Elgers and Dean Harry Allan have been generous in their discussions and criticisms. Stephen Demski interupted his own work to go over the typescript and induce me to make changes I had not considered. My debt to him is great. Edward Horn, a naturalist by profession, argued many points with me, and is owed my gratitude. Mrs Vesta Powers and her able straff have worried over my impossible scrawl and produced a readable typescript. Ms Joyce Sicard of that staff took over the final typing with great expedition. Ms Elizabeth Wark, my graduate assistant took over most of the task of preparing the galleys for publication. Finally my wife, Irene, listened to my thoughts and infrequently expressed doubt or surprise. All these I thank.

January 1989

Sidney C. Sufrin
School of Management
University of Massachusetts
Amherst, Massachuseetts

Chapter I
Ethics, Markets and Policy

1 Choice is the Basis

It all starts with wants and resources. Put another way, the social function of any economy is essentially to provide for its members. Since providing income and security is not achieved by unthinking processes, by merely following the dictates of nature in some Rousseauean fashion, choice is implicit in personal behavior as well as social behavior. This should not be taken to mean that all things are possible to people as individuals or as a society. All things are possible only in a grand theological sense. Even in this grand sense theologians have raised the question, "Does God do what He does because it is right, or is it right because God does it?" But such profundities and mysteries are not the subject to our more modest inquiry.

We are concerned with the structure and the content of what is called ethical and policy formulation in the context of an economy or market system. So long as there are choices, or the illusion of choices, so long as people think and act as if there are alternatives of thinking and acting, questions of degrees of goodness and badness, however conceived and measured, are implicit in thought and action. People say "There is a wrong way and a right way". What do they mean? I take it that the right way is the more technically and/or socially efficient way to accomplish the task. All other ways are less desirable to the person making the observation. Others may disagree. Their disagreement is either technical or moral, or possibly, both.

In small matters both technique and morality may be unimportant. Frying an egg is not an earthshaking matter. Yet there are alternative techniques favored by one or another person. And morality may enter if the egg is fried in bacon grease and passed off to an orthodox Muslim or Jew as merely a fried egg.

On the other hand having a leaky roof repaired may involve a more considered judgment as to technique and morality. Price sharpens the judgmental process. What kind of sheathing, what grade of tar paper, what kind of shingle are price and technical considerations. But the way the roofing market is administered may be a price-moral question. Is there price fixing? Do competitors really compete? Are the assurances based on experimental facts or are they mere words? The cost of the roof repair brings to consciousness alternative techniques and issues of morality or honesty. Doubtless the roofer wonders about the honesty of the customer. Will he pay the bill without a squawk; Will the check be good? Will the customer, if dissatisfied, spread ruinous stories about the roofer?

Some moral and technical aspects of behavior are controlled against becoming general issues by law, licensing, custom, good will and common sense on the part to both roofer and householder. The very ongoingness of business makes transactions usually smooth and routine. If the householder, in the heat of a summer's day, brings a pitcher of lemonade to the roofer, the act is a good one. It is even a species of an ethical action, although admittedly minor. The householder has freely given a cooling drink to a person exposed to the rays of the sun. The accent is on freely. The roofer is not expected to pay in any way for the lemonade, nor is he expected to act in any especially thankful way. The act is one of politeness and concern. If the roofer were given a bicycle for his son, then more than mere politeness may be involved.

Whether or not the householder had a self interest motive in the lemonade or the bicycle is not a major problem. Feeling good, making space in the garage, showing off, may all be among the householder's motives. They however are part of a transcendental transfer between roofer and customer, but they are not part of the explicit money-service exchange. That exchange was a market not a transcendental happening. Money was paid for service and materials. The transaction was contractual in the ordinary sense of the word. All else was ex market, was setting. The setting of course is important to an understanding of an action. But it is the scene of the action, not the action. Does it have a bearing on the action? Often, probably usually. But the setting, the scene of the action, can be distinguished from the action, for it is the latter which is the transaction of importance, the action of exchange.

2 Money is the Nub

Markets may be defined as the exchange process. The constraints and restraints of the process inevitably have an effect on the efficiency of the market system. The market system, in its macro or aggregate view, is the mode by which scarce resources are put to work producing income, and by which the income is distributed. However the units doing the work of production and receiving the income produced-units of the ownership of land, capital and the individuals of entrepreneurship and labor are micro units. Employment, unemployment income and their distribution can be viewed as either micro or macro phenomena. Individuals are employed, partially employed, or unemployed; and individuals receive little or a great deal of money income, thus having varying claims on goods and services. On the other hand employment or unemployment may be high or low generally. An unemployment rate of 5 % may be the index of a good state of affairs for a society. But for the unemployed, as individuals and families, the situation is bad.[1]

The upshot of these observations is that the wholeness – the gestalt of the impressions and observations about the market system becomes understandable only if somehow the micro and macro aspects are unified and synthesized. Such synthesis has been a nagging, unresolved problem of recent and current economic theorizing. Ever since Keynes proposed what, in effect, is the macro role in determining micro levels and decisions, the problem of a theoretical synthesis between micro and macro systems has been a challenge.

3 Constancy Thy Name is not Society

But the "real" world, that is to say the activities of the market system – not an abstract market system but the ongoing economic system – has not sought nor achieved any neat fitting together of the parts of the system to conform to the bigger social system. Such an idea that the market system is a picture puzzle whose general configuration and parts are determined, and the two determined components all fit together, such an idea is utterly foreign to social behavior. Rather the configuration of the general system is not viewed as determined, and the parts are also not determined. The whole system – general boundaries and parts, all are adjustable, changeable, malleable and also added and subtracted as the result of many forces and factors. Social laws are not so constant as physical laws.

Nor is the idea of efficiency a static one. Trade offs based on changing values, changing knowledge, new issues and new fads and fashions of behavior are the very spirit of an ongoing social system which comprehends both micro and macro aspects. The interaction of micro and macro, of small and large entities in the market-business system has to do, in an operational sense, with changes in the structure of markets. Technology is developed in the laboratories or in the minds of effective people. Micro changes happen, e.g. new computers with varying capacities, new drugs, changed clothing and food fashions, new ways to get control of a company, new ways to raise money for investment, etc. ad infinitum.

The social system is not static. That is not to say that everything is changing all the time. Change is uneven. It is slow in some areas, rapid in others. Ways to collect taxes, educate young people, make steel, sell food, as examples, do not change much overnight or in a decade. On the other side of the coin, some banking practices, medical costs, military expenditures, short term interest rates, and foreign investments do not take long to change.

We live in a time in which many private values and ideologies are being nominated for and some treated as if they are public values.

In the U.S. abortion as an evil is being pushed as a candidate for legislated illegitimation or even constitutional legitimation. Homosexuality and the civil rights of homosexuals, budgetary deficits, aspects of protection against currently defined improper search and seizure, the abrogation of certain aspects of international law related to supporting revolutionary foreign activity in times of peace, and business behavior at many levels are among issues for which some legislative or Constitutional legitimation is being sought in the face of an obvious split in the current, social legitimating agreement.

All the changes which are the result of market forces and perceptions of market forces are driven by some idea of efficieny. The micro units-firms, governments, consumers as examples, operate so as to achieve some desired goals as cheaply and effectively as they know how.

Efficiency however is not the only goal of the several actors in the market. As Herbert Simon and his school teach us, people have more than one goal, and they seek often to "satisfice" rather than maximize the profits of an activity. By less than maximizing, but nevertheless achieving some desired level of gain, other determined goals may be achieved. Trade offs are endemic. The market is, in such cases, not the scene of maximization of a given variable e.g. profits, so much as it is the scene in which a number of goals are sought, the level of the several achievements being, in a sense, a trade off among the goals. In such cases efficiency is not the gaining of a single goal, which is to be maximized, but the gaining of a complex of ends. [2]

So far the motives and restraints are self generated, the micro actors are each seeking goals which, in most instances probably, are identical or nearly so – e.g. profits, risk aversion, stability. The means that often intricate patterns of behavior, are also often similar or even identical. The micro system is building up to a macro system. But then market intervention occurs.

Government, to gain some goal or goals it believes desirable and attainable, may act to change the structure of the market. Such policy is limited by the compromises necessary to enact a law, by the knowledge and administrative skill of the administration and courts, and by the ideology of compromises which are at the base of the conception of what the goals of policy should be. The result of the government intervention is to change the structure and performance of markets.

The anti trust ideology is one which supports competition as the market ideal against monopoly and oligopoly. The choice is not only, nor even mainly, because competition assures a bigger output at lower prices than degrees of competition. Freedom is what is ultimately involved. Anti trust also assumes that a market system of competition preserves and assures more fairness for potential competitors to "enter and do business" than less competitive systems; that control of markets by one or a few firms tends to stifle technological change, that politically a freer market is more conducive to a free democracy than a less free system. In other words the economics of anti trust is inextricably bound to other goals.

Administrative incursions are of many varieties. Some examples are:

(1) By such interventions as wage-hour regulation, anti trust, various tax laws, pure food and drug requirements, anti pollution controls, and so on efficiency for the micro units may be and usually is restricted. Macro efficiency presumably viewed as socially desirable changes is advanced and improved. Lack of knowledge, analytic failure and synthetic miscalculation, all limitations on rationality, cause results unlike what was wanted to occur. (2) Administrative and judicial interpretation also often tend to make the results assumed in the original plans and formulations become something different when results are examined. A third factor (3) causing the results to differ from the anticipations is due to the micro actors changing their goals and actions in the light of the interventions. This last

element is the basis for the theory of rational expectations and the hypothesis of efficient markets which argue that government intervention can often (usually) be minimized because of the insights and technical skill of the micro actors.

It is clear from what we have asserted that issues of social ethics, which incorporate ideas of justice and fairness, are at the basis of technical intervention by government into market structure. Indeed if there were no ethical reason and purpose for changing market behavior, the sole consideration of legislature, courts and administrators would be a technical concern to improve efficiency. Macro efficiency would be merely the sum of micro efficiencies. This is obviously a very limited way to evolve government intervention, for intervention almost always, or (we feel) generally implies a cost to someone and a gain to someone else. Such costs and gains flow from the intervention. Social welfare is not merely the sum of private welfares, and private welfares are rarely changed without gains and losses reverberating throughout the market system.

A concern for economic welfare including both the social and individual welfare is as old as human *society, and surely even older*. The period from say, 1550 in Western Europe is considered a reasonable starting point for the modern treatment of political, economic and social welfare. The Mercantilists, the early worldly philosophers of France and Great Britain, including those secular saints as Locke, Hume, Smith and Ricardo, and their followers into the present day, see the strong relationship between markets on the one hand and social welfare on the other.[3]

The past 30 or so years have seen a remarkable reorientation of the social ideal. From the great revolutionary period of the 18th century the social ideal has been progress. Progress is difficult to define. Most clearly it means an increase in personal freedom, in social liberty, in the enhancement of the arts and sciences, in responsive and responsible government as well as an improvement in the income, and in security and dignity of people in and out of the work place. In recent years, however, probably during the Johnson Administration and surely as an index of the Reagan ideal, progress has been reduced to growth, meaning economic growth. This is an ethical retrogression. Yet the Johnson term of office is probably more notable for social reform and action than for growth. The surge of the past persisted but is declining.

Adherent to the growth view, conservatives tend to believe that market efficiency engenders social and political progress. Liberals, adherent to the progress view, tend to believe that conscious even planned intervention is required by government to assure growth. The liberty and freedom aspects, insofar as they are good in their own right, too require social i.e. governmental support. Neither side, conservative nor liberal, seems devoted to any particular ideology with respect to art and science, although there probably are differences to be seen if one looks hard enough.

The tendency for economic conservatives also to be social conservatives, and economic liberals to be social liberals, I believe, is fairly obvious. This relationship obtains not universally but with sufficient frequency to permit a rough and ready classification of people and movements. By *conservative* in economic theory I mean reliance on classical and traditional, equilibirial oriented economics. The great names in this tradition extend from Smith to Friedman and Debreu, from Ricardo to Marshall and Pigou to Stigler and Hayek.

In politics, which is the arena in which the various views of social ethics are exhibited for all to see, Reagan is a late 20th Century spokesman (along with Margaret Thatcher in Great Britain) for conservatism but the name of Herbert Hoover in the earlier part of the 20th century is a milestone. The Adams family earlier in the Nation's history and Cal Coolidge at the end of an era are also landmark names in conservatism. The policies and program of each differ because the issues differed. The ideologies were the same, in great part, namely *laisser faire.*

Economic *liberals,* in the current sense of the word, start with the premise that the macro economic system does not work with automatic efficiency. The greatest proof is the existence of involuntary unempolyment over extended periods of time. Other imbalances, as in foreign trade, unstable price levels, unsold stocks as in agriculture, etc. illustrate the observation. The micro system, on the whole, less a concern of the Keynesian liberals, nevertheless must be faced. In this, however, there is the tendency to stay within the confines of traditional theory. How to synthesize micro and macro is indeed a mystery to the liberals. We may add that the conservative synthesis is not convincing. Samuelson, Galbraith, Tobin and Solow are American important liberal economists.

The times and the circumstances elicit solutions which, for time and circumstances, can be classified as generally liberal or conservative. In a general way, both Conservatives and Liberals supported the Anti Trust movement of the turn of the century. Some business interests, and ideologically left wing groups, e.g. Socialists, probably felt that large scale business activity was either desirable or inevitable. Big business was potientially threatened by attacks on size as monopolistic, but must have also recognized that market control by private interests made market control by government easier than if markets were competitive.

Currently anti trust has become an ideological commonplace, although precisely what criteria are appropriate to define market control are unresolved issues both theoretically and practically.

The application of a social ethic, is operationally stymied by both technical and specific value confusions and lack of clarity. Can either liberals or conservatives really tell what the results are of permitting or denying a merger, say, of Brown Shoe and Kinney? Each was relatively small in the whole scheme of shoe manufacture and distribution, but each had carved a niche for itself and was well situated. In Brown Shoe Co. vs. U.S. (370-U.S.-294) the Supreme Court held in 1962 that the merger "may tend to lessen competition substantially in the retail sale of men's, women's and children's shoes" and affirmed that the merger was in violation of law. That was in 1962.

By 1985 all sorts of running shoes, sneakers, and athletic shoes were widely used in ordinary wear. Scarcely a child or young adult does not wear such shoes a good part of the time. By 1985 imports of Italian, Czech, Spanish and other shoes were more commonly used than in 1962.

Would a decision made now be the same as the original one? Is the current organization of the shoe industry a result of the very powerful Brown Shoe case? Twenty or thirty years is not a long time in the operation and development of an industry, yet pretty clearly the past 2 or 3 decades have been a prologue to the present. Therefore how does one, a liberal or a conservative, sitting on the bench or arguing before the bar, or preparing an economic analytic brief for a lawyer, know what the rule being propounded or developed implies?

Yet courts, lawyers and economists cannot sit on their hands and do nothing when an issue requires resolution in the opinion of someone with authority. Action is not only indicated, it is required. So, we might remark parenthetically, is a good measure of humility and caution. But ultimately judgment must be relied on to approve argument, analysis and persuasion. The liberal-conservative biases and differences become less meaningful in the light of the uncertainties of future history, and the hidden and unknown weaknesses in analysis and synthesis.

Decisions, then, inevitably tend to be particularistic even if legitimated as being general and in accord with some idealized set of principles. On the whole liberals and conservatives, who may perceive events differently come from the same social, historical and ideolgical setting. Income is implicitly desired as a good in growth, as is equity, justice, fariness, progress, individualism, and so endlessly on. What these goals and ideals mean to each person is, of course, different. However, as time runs its historic course, there tend to be groupings of people around certain ideas and ideals often associated with great current issues.

The Great Depression which began in 1929 was a time of liberal and conservative bunching along the social spectrum. What was liberal or conservative in 1929 or 1935 is not precisely liberal or conservative in 1985. Mondale knew this when he unsuccessfully ran for President, and so do the organizations which supported him. Compassion, a buzz word in 1960 or even 1970, did not have much appeal in 1984 or 1988.

4 Reason vs. Logic

Now to get to the nub of the problem. Argument tries to be persuasive, it tries to secure the approval and accord of those to whom it is directed. This may be done by logic, appeals to experience or by playing on the emotions of the target person or persons. The emotional appeal, although widely used, is no substitute for rationality or reason. Rationality includes in its meaning logical, sensible and reasonable. Logical argument is limited by its assumptions and by its static nature. Sensible or reasonable argument, on the other hand, is generally taken to include such elements as changed or changing assumptions due to experience or anticipated experience. In other words a reasonable position or expectation of events is not so rigid nor linear as a logical argument. Reasonable, sensible arguments on a large enough scale also have the saving grace of legitimating achievable goals. This is not an infallible nor possibly even a usual rule. But all of us have experienced, personally and socially, the phenomenon of self fulfilling prophesies.

The managers of a firm, for whatever personal or corporate motives, donate a gift to the opera or for some foreign relief program. The web of implications become socially desirable in the minds of many, even most, observers because the action is seen as a worthy undertaking. Those, who on the sidelines mutter that the business of business is business, miss the point. What they really are asserting is that the business of business *should be* business. They are moralists not mere observers. But those who applaud the action, too, are moralists. They are saying "right on" to an action which presumably does *not* create profits, but requires profits as a means.

Social morality, in our view is the legitimation of behavior, private or public. Behavior required by law or custom is often legitimated if there is conformity. But decisive tests of legitimation of behavior, private or public, *departs* from the requirement of the norm. No one seriously complains that Jefferson's purchase of the Louisiana territory was immoral, or that Lincoln's Proclamation deprived innocent, non belligerent individuals of their slave property. In current experience, the concern over the Salvadoran and Nicaraguan political situations is a case in point of the wispy nature of legitimation. The CIA had prepared a handbook on counter insurgency for El Salvador which outlines techniques of terror based on the selective murder of civilian officials who were considered less than loyal, or whose murders would be blamed on the insurgents who would thereby be denegrated. There was an outcry against the document in the U.S. as well as the defending argument that war is hell, and government (U.S.?, Salvadoran?) should do what it could to win the war. A few months later *insurgents* in El Salvador were accused of murdering local officials. The ascribed motives were – as one might guess – to cast blame on the insurgents and terrorize the population. The legitimations, in the minds of many including editorial writers, was quite opposite to that of government's murdering or insurgent's assassinating people. The genesis of the bifurcation clearly is ideological.

In less bloodthirsty circumstances, we suggest that the, or at least a, root of conservative thought – or individualism as an unsullied, uncontaminated ideal, is implicit in micro economic analysis with its assumption of an ideal competition as the pure theory. This ideology is transferred to the macro system, which becomes, in a sense, the sum of the micro markets. No one takes such analysis seriously as a good image of reality. It remains a *moral* ideal related to income maximization. *Real* i.e. quantitative and physical deviations from the ideal are treated as the result of obstacles to the realization of the ideal. Such analysis and synthesis are clearly ideological and moral rather than scientific.

In economics the liberal view is similarly ideological. Individualism, however is tempered by less than perfect knowledge and by "animal spirits" (a psychological phenomenon Keynes discovered somewhere, and which seemingly is based on the theory that man is lower than angels but higher than animals). In more normal language animal spirits becomes the propensity for risk taking.

At the macro level, which is not a sum of the micro units, for to assume such would be to commit the fallacy of composition, at the macro level the micro anticipations and actions *interact* and do not neatly conform to each other. The interactions may well cause business to fluctuate. The surprise is not that we have business cycles and general economic disturbances.

The surprise is that such distortions do not occur more often. Neatness and smoothness are characteristics neither of private nor social life. A task of the social scientist, presumably, is to analyze such lack of harmony.

Both the conservative and the liberal schools of economics and business then have the same task. It is in their preconceptions of ideology – of values in action and of what ought to be-that they differ. If we are correct in this, a logical or reasonable synthesis of micro and macro economics or micro and macro anything else in the realm of ordered analysis and synthesis is not to be found in any of the social disciplines. It is to be sought in reflections on ideology. Such synthesis has its roots in politics and morality not in economic models and statistics.[4]

5 The Whole is not the Sum of the Parts

An observation regarding social structure seems in order. Organizations are classified in many ways, all of which are designed to provide some insight into how they operate. One is to consider organizations of people as either associatively or communally oriented. The latter class of organizations are held together by bonds of loyalty, common purpose and ideals of service to society or to defined groups. Churches may need money and have money raising functions. But money raising is not, and, in the minds of most people, should not be the major function of a church. Service to the society, community, indeed for the Deity, are the ideal goals. And the membership is, supposedly, bound to each other by the common ideals. Ritual as a way to become prepared for the acceptance of and dedication to the ideals becomes a significant mode of group binding. This is also true for fraternal organizations, aberrant political groups, especially revolutionary groups and from time to time appears in colleges and universities. General purpose and coherence mark out the communal organizations. It is not strange that such organizations, if successful, tend to generate or at least foster strong directive even charismatic leaders. Such leadership may go beyond reasonable persuasion and lyrical appeal, using brute force and terror to secure adherence to policy and program. Such communal organizations are typically not economic in the modern world.[5] Jones, of the Jonesville catastrophe, is an example of one who used ignoble persuasion and force to manage a society which he then destroyed.

The corporation, partnership and individual and family undertaking are generally viewed as associations of people concerned with self benefit or interest. Partnerships and family operations may often tend to be less individually oriented since the personal relations between and among the acting persons is often not merely impersonal and income oriented. Sons tend to treat fathers differently from the way they deal with non relations. But corporations *qua* corporations are in business to make money, and in major matters people in corporations act that way. Leadership is recognized if it is successful, and success means income or wealth aggrandizement or stability in an unstable world. The roles of violence, loyalty, and public service are not stressed. Now as corporations become the dominant form of business enterprise, and as welfare becomes a pressing social concern, the entry of business into the welfare scene is not surprising. It is part of the legitimation process. Similarly as communal organizations become large and costly they tend to act more like bankers than they did in the past. Big hospitals are more profit oriented than small endowed or privately supported hospitals.

As government becomes larger and as its welfare functions become suspect, first because in the aggregate they are costly, and second because examples of operational failure are not hard to find, government tries to step back. "Balance the budget," "Get the government off our backs," Reagan's and Carter's running against Washington and the bureaucracy, are U.S. symbols of the late 20th Century. Individualism and government responsibility, meaning lower taxes and a balanced budget, while still providing "needed", i.e. proper but undefined social services, are a current, social legitimating wave. We want a "safety net" to catch failure before it is too costly.

Charity, i.e. gifts and grants based on a freely willed devotion to public service and common good, is the obvious way to cut publicly provided social services. This, however, is true only by logic. Whether or not the private sector will, infact, respond is, in our expectations, not a difficult question to answer. The associative, corporate bodies lack the ideology and internal support to attempt the coodinated undertaking of welfare. And if they did, which is most unlikely, would it be socially acceptable? Would the owners, the share holders agree? Can a democratic, which is to say ultimately communal society, allow welfare and welfare policy to be made by associative bodies? On this issue most conservatives and most liberals would agree.

In the current American world the ideolgical tendency surely from the F.D.R. New Deal until the Carter and Reagan administrations has been to give great weight to the intervention aspects of government as securing at least two goals:

1 improving the social welfare condition by protecting weak economic groups and transferring income to them, and
2 counteracting tendencies of markets to falter and reduce the flow of income, and not allowing relative prices or price levels to change in fashions believed to reduce social welfare.

A third goal, often subsumed under the other two, but probably sufficiently important to warrant its own classification, is:

3 benefitting some particular groups in the economy, e.g. farmers, unprofitable industries, minorities.

The conservative ideal, currently exemplified by market deregulation policy, the soft pedalling of anti trust and anti segregation policies, falls into three classes of means.

1 market deregulation e.g. anti trust, subsidy, and tax reform
2 softening protective legislation and enforcement for defined groups e.g. affirmative action, minimum wages, medicaid, social security and aid to education.
3 By default or design, weakening state and local intervention, should localities and states desire to fill the vacuum resluting from federal policies. (The 1986 tax reform of the Reagan administration.)

The pre and post Carter-Reagan philosophies of government obviously differ just as the economic theoretical approaches differ. The events which assumed a social watershed dimension was, in my view, the social upheaval of the 1960s and 70s. If a book and a name are to be associated with the change they are *The Greening of America* by C.A. Reich. The book was a plea for a new way to look at the social world. Reich's celebrated Consciousness III was for *individuals* to be concerned with those interests which the economic and organizational parts of society have failed to supply.[6] Reich's appeal gained an enormous response. He appealed to the individual, and individualism had attained an enormous popularity and recognition in the 60s and thereafter. The appeal was also to reform commonly held values, or better inculcate new values into old institutions. In a youthful world of even moderately educated and self conscious people, this was a welcome appeal. The bridge between individual interest and social concern was built and builded on; leading ultimately to support of the young, urban upwardly mobile professionals for Senator Hart in the 1984 presidential primaries.

This social structure however did not bridge the gap between the Conservative and Liberal economists and policy makers. They remained locked in verbal and equational combat.

The alternate views of the conflicting camps, on the theoretic, competitive level may be conveniently encapsulated by crudely expressing them as:

1 *Conservative* – if governmental and other interventions which restrict the efficiency of markets were excised the result would be a strong tendency for income and employment nevertheless to tend toward oprimization, and economic growth assured (efficient market hypothesis). There is no unanimity as to precisely what steps would lead to this happy state of affairs. (1) Monetarists would limit increases in money supply by some formulas. (2)Supply siders would reduce taxes, the new classicists would restrict government regulation and some monopolistic tendencies, and so on. The diverse programs may, in a general way, be classified, as libertarian, individualistic, and from our particularistic point of view, as relying on markets and market forces, arising from some "natural" or self generating force or tendency, to direct the economy to more socially desired goals than exogenously directed forces and tendencies would. This view seems to me to be Adam Smith's invisible hand.

Is there an invisible hand (self interest) or is the invisible hand an "as if" analogy as: people in markets acting to satisfy their interests, act *as if* they were directed by an invisible hand. In other words, is there a natural something, a hidden spring, which leads people in markets to seek their own interest and find the welfare of the society? If there is, then the free market supplies the mechanism for synthesizing the micro and macro theoretical economic systems. How this synthesis is accomplished remains if not a mystery, an unproved proposition.

Whether the economists we classify as conservative embrace, generally speaking, a conservative public policy because of their theorizing, or whether the conservative stance tends to appeal to certain people is an unanswered question. But the several brands of conservative do seem related. This is not a new phenomenon. How many socially conservative Marxists are there?

2 *Liberal.* The liberal economic views, especially those related to the Keynesian doctrine, tend, generally speaking, to be related to a concern for perceived social problems as unemployment, poverty, old age, etc. From the economic theoretical viewpoint this class of economists do not see markets, if unfettered by intervention, producing and *distributing* income

in any ideal fashion. These economists see booms and busts as inherent in markets. They see wages (between 2/3 and 3/4 of the G.N.P.) as not set by informed and possibly correct ideas of self interest but by other perceptions. They see prices and wages often as "sticky" that is not freely and quickly adjusting to market signals, they see money as more diversified in its market dimensions than merely, in gross, regulating levels of output and employment. In short government intervention is necessary if some kind of stability and decency is to be attained.

For these economists the micro system and the macro system are not automatically and inevitably synthesized into a unity. They are made compatible or better, the macro system is made effective, by intervention. Markets and market behavior are not "natural," they are social.

Clearly we have made our divisions too sharp. But the tendency we believe to be correct. If one had to make a generalization about conservatives and liberals in public policy and economic theorizing, one might assert, admitting that the generalization was not entirely true for every case but as a tendency, that Conservatives see the market process and many related social processes as tending toward results which are both ethical and effective i.e. efficient. Liberals tend to see market and social processes tending toward implications which need be particularistically judged as to their ethics and effectiveness. Where judgment is not satisfied with both or either, intervention is indicated, hence justified if it works. The kindliness of nature is more likely to be assumed by conservatives than liberals. Liberals tend to be more critical of what is, being interested in what might be.[7]

It should be emphasized that both liberal and conservative thought and behavior in the U.S. have many traits in common. Individualism, constitutionalism, social mobility, progress and so on are common to both. Their opposites are repugnant to both. But in ways and means to achieve ends, in the *particular* ends sought in *particular* cases there are differences. That liberals seem more in a hurry than conservatives who are willing to wait for the "long run" of economics to set matters straight. How long can society or an individual wait is, however, often a vital issue.

6 Market Ethics and Ethics in the Market

As we suggest, the period since roughly 1975 has seen a great public debate on the economic policy of the U.S. After Watergate and its exposures, business ethics became a great issue in public debate. Questions concering the justification of "whistle blowing", issues of canons of ethics for business, business bribery and malfeasance, and so on, were publicly debated. Business or market ethics evolve as does any question of behavior. Person A behaves in a certain fashion so that persons B, C ... N are affected. Questions of the motives of A arise, and of the nature of the act. Of great importance to those involved are the effects. In other words the moral and substantive effects require legitimation if the action is to be judged ethically. Since A, the actor, is assumed to be motivated and to make a choice prior to his action, the person A must be a real, live person not merely a corporation or other artificial body. People are not firms.

The essence of an exchange is that A and B trade money for a good or service. Each one presumably acts freely, within a market structure. If the buyer is buying a complex, dangerous, or risky product the market structure may require information, warnings, limitations on sale to protect the buyer against untoward implications; or should do so, in the liberal viewpoint.

The conservative viewpoint is possibly less insistent on direct restraints, but the conservative would suggest that if the buyer is not satisfied not only will he/she not buy the product a second time, but his/her experience will be transmitted to other buyers. The implications therefore provide self correction to sellers. Ethics are not an issue, except in the sense that the structure of the market reflects an ethical interest. Purchase and sale then are less ethically supervised than structurally supervised by the market. Ethics is a hidden force in the market. This point of view is not a micro one so much as it is a macro-market view.

Ethics, in the market however, as a direct factor in the relations between A and B, C ... N would come into play if A simply makes an offer to B ... N, without any price, although other conditions may be set. If you are under 25, a high school graduate, have worked for the company for 5 years you may apply for a tuition grant for college. Ostensibly such an offer comes from a company. In reality it comes from someone or some committee acting in the name of the company, but is not part of the market activities of any one. It is, pure and simple, an offer without any money consideration. It is an act presumably of goodness. Its implications of course may be to improve labor relations or community relations, or be a species of subsidized training and education. But it is not wise to examine the mouth of the gift horse too closely. It is, we argue, the irrelevance of money as an exchange trade off which marks personal ethics in the market, or elsewhere.

In the discussions which are so frequent in news media, books and on television and radio, the ethics of business and markets are not so much concerned with nonmarket behavior as a concern with the *legality* or appropriateness of market behavior. Was the law broken, was it properly interpreted, was there a law to be broken, should there have been a law? Such questions are asked about whistle blowing, industrial bribery, and shoddy, dangerous goods sold to unsuspecting buyers. The arguments often are a mixture of ethical considerations and legal considerations. That the two are related is beyond cavil in spite of Justice Holmes' wisecrack about not seeking justice in the law. The *law is the haven of justice, fairness and responsibility.* These are aspects of ethics until they are written into law and become a rule.

Rules are not ethical because ethics, as we define or see it, presupposes a freely willed choice by the actor. Honesty is the best policy is a moral maxim if it suggests being honest is a good in itself. The statement is a managerial maxim if it means that business success is more likely if one is honest than if one is dishonest. Franklin's Poor Richard was teasing us by giving us an aphorism about honesty being the best policy which could please either liberal or conservative. What he really meant we can never know.

Rule, as we have asserted, whether law or strong convention, whether statute, or common law decision, contains ethical underpinnings in its formulation. But once in being, rule is a requirement, actions however which do not meet our ethical definition, which includes the idea of actions freely chosen when there are possible alternatives, may become legitimated in their own right and so become new rules. Thus there are unlikely to be definite rules about whistle blowing, while there can be and are more definite rules about bribery and conspiracy.

A whistle blower who exposes a nefarious action, or a waste of federal money or a minor peccadillo, must be judged by the seriousness and the implications of what he or she exposes. To trumpet that the Boss hired his incompetent son-in-law and thereby to ruin the Boss's reputation is small potatoes. Indeed the whistle act is so small and mean as to possibly be an unethical act, if the implications are serious for company and Boss. But if the Boss stole $500,000 or bribed a government official, the whistle blowing act would be ethical. Had the whistle blower a reasonable opportunity to bring the issue to the attention of authority without going public becomes an issue in judging the act. That the Boss was a miscreant is admitted. *How* was he exposed is the issue. This example distinguishes between the exposure and the crime, between non legal and legal behavior.

In questions of market ethics as a personal matter, I suggest that the law and the nonlegal aspects must be distinguished. That ethical behavior to do a good deed or expose a bad one is outside the market is essential. Legality and efficiency are separate judgments.[8] Being a good person is not restrained by law. Being a bad person may be.

The lawful-unlawful category is related to the efficient-inefficient categories. Laws, as we suggest which affect the market and its structure often are made so as to gain other ends than market efficiency. The social and private values of full efficiency are believed by legislature, administrators and courts to be less than the social and private amenities which the law requires or protects. Thus social ethics are often enactments. The Common Law performs the same function to the degree the courts incorporate into decisions the ideologies of the society. To the extent that courts generally are sensitive to public values as well as to statutory requirement, the courts are living in the great tradition of the Common Law.

On the way to approach global or macro issues the liberals and conservatives differ. We may, however, divide the philosophic approaches to great social issues into three not only two categories. The third category we should add is the religious. The ideal type is not The Moral Majority for it has managed to commingle, not to say synthesize American populism and American evangelical fundamentalism. In our view the evangelical fundamentalism of America is often built around charismatic leaders (e. g. Billy Sunday, Jerry Falwell, Billy Graham) whose interpretation of scripture or whose evaluation of policy and behavior may be idiosyncratic. The social policies typically supported by such groups are often conservative. However, while on personal matters as "right to life" or homosexuality they tend to be conservative, the ranks probably would break on aid to farmers or curtailment of social security benefits. On such matters the populism might well shine forth and lead to a traditional liberal position.

It is the Catholic Bishops that we shall consider the ideal religious type. Not because the Bishops take a persistent liberal or conservative view. But unlike the Moral Majority position, the Bishops follow an *organized religious position of relying on rule* not ethics. Ethics is buried in the rule, it is not manifested by free choice on particular issues or particular circumstances. Abortion, homosexuality, care for the poor and needful, nuclear war and armaments, relations between employer and employee, such personal and micro issues are resolved by adherence to rules the Bishops find in accord with Church teachings and dogma. The Moral Majority are probably more particularistic than the Bishops. Like the Moral Majority the Bishops are neither strongly liberal or conservative. Nor do they particularly stand for ethical judgment after the rule is made. The rule embodies the ethic, but from then on, it is a rule to be followed as a duty.

We comment on the religious contribution to current ethical structure because for some reasons not clear to the writer, the religious inputs to public policy have been more consistent in recent years than in the past, if not particularly novel in content.

We are left with the Liberals and Conservatives.

An ideal type person on the Conservative wing, although one among several, is George Gilder – a professional writer on social issues, trained in sociology. His *Wealth and Poverty* (1980) created a stir among Conservatives because here was an obvious intellectual who could write well and was dedicated to defending the traditional conservative economic position. He was more interesting than William Buckley who tended to look down his nose at friend and foe, who was an egg head not merely an intellectual, and besides has just about worn out his welcome on T.V. and radio. Like liberal Kenneth Galbraith, Buckley was old hat by 1980. Also Buckley tended to use formal logical arguments to prove propositions, arguments which often were artificial, abstract and verbose. (I freely grant that my personal bias guides my hand.) Gilder, on the other hand, was simple, concrete and historical. He gives examples and numbers.

The *Spirit of Enterprise* is a good example of the Gilder way. The thesis is simple: People run themselves and the world. Successful people make a successful world, and Americans can do it because they have done it before. Americans who have "know how", the spirit of enterprise, guts, willingness to take a chance in making frozen fried potatoes or complex computer components will prevail. The clear implication is that personal drive leads to success and this is fair and just.

Just how the drive of A affects B . . . N who have less drive, know how, moxie, etc. is not well developed. In our language the micro and macro systems are not synthesized. The reader must supply the argument that the invisible hand (which is knowledge, experience and talent) guides the willing if less able along the path broken by the more able. Just how this results in income maximization or optimization, in a steady circuit flow of income and cost and in stability is not revealed. To those already convinced or who do not see the problems, Gilder is convincing. His heartiness, upbeat outlook and obvious enjoyment in his work make him a natural Conservative pundit. Ethical questions for him are not at issue. More is better than less and markets are efficient if one would only use them (properly).

As much as one (the writer in this instance) is attracted to Gilder, by that much the reader (again the writer) finds him exciting but unconvincing, readable but forgettable.

For the liberal ideal type, again one among several, we choose Lester Thurow of MIT. Thurow is a trained economist, a (proto? post?) Keynesian who has served a stint on the N.Y. Times as editorial writer, is a frequent contributor to the press and T.V., and has an exciting tone in his writing. He also gives the distinct impression of being comfortable with economic analysis and his vast inventory of carefully selected facts. As Gilder has replaced Buckley, Thurow has replaced Galbraith as the liberal who speaks out. With Robert Heilbronner, Thurow has written *The Economic Problem,* a college text. That Heilbronner is the other author is interesting because he is one of the thoughtful socialists of academia as well as the popular press. This does not make Thurow a Socialist (not that that would be a mark against him) but it does illustrate that Thurow is not devoted to depending or protecting any social or economic institution merely because it is in place.

In his *Generating Inequality*[10] Thurow faces a problem (income distribution) which, while popular 30 years or so ago, has not been recently sufficiently considered when he wrote the book. Yet the distribution of income is obviously, from the viewpoint of welfare, quite as important as the size of the income to be distributed. For Thurow income distribution is an important part of the question of equity. Equity is generally defined as meeting conditions of justice (not well defined), ideology, and welfare (size and distribution of the national product (p. 23). The remainder of the work is devoted to presenting information on income generation and distribution (a task the author obviously enjoys) and suggesting ways and means of attaining an equitable and effective distribution of income.

This is not the place to go into the details of Thurow's policy suggestions. His mode of attack, however is interesting, and persistent in his later work. He defines a problem and works out a solution. The problem and the solution are not general. That is to say he doesn't go in for *general* or large scale planning and intervention. His interventionism rather is specifically directed at what he considers an immediate issue and its close implications or connections. In this he is safely in line with the Keynsian or other interventionistic programs of the American tradition. He is, in fact, in the line of Galbraith, Commons and J.M. Clark. Whether or not one agrees with Thurow, the issues are fairly laid out, and the ethical content which guides his policy advice is obvious. Thus he opens himself to criticism by his economist colleagues who do not like his technical analysis. His ethical preconceptions do not invite criticism because they are the definitions of his concern. To argue over them would be merely to substitute one set of definitions for another. Those who would take on this task must engage in a metaphysical, philosophical discussion, an area economists try to avoid except in the discussion of methodology, which occur about once in a generation.

The discussion leads us to some observations about ethics, markets and policy:

1 Policy, whether law, near law or ideology always contains considerations of ethics – of The Good.
2 Private ethics is not an economic activity in the first instance, although it often has economic implications.
3 Obedience to law, custom or strong idelogy is not an ethical phenomenon.
4 Observance of religious rules is not ethical, it is observance of rule or dogma.
5 Liberals seek usually to solve fairly well defined problems in the light of ideologies which are not always clearly expressed. Once the particular rules of problem solving are in place, there is no need for ethical judgment. The ethics is in the rule. Therefore, Liberals do not rely on ethics in an ongoing situation.
6 Conservatives, implicitly assuming that markets (and other institutions) are efficient, tend to rely on the institutions, not on interference with them. Markets (and other institutions) work. Ethics then is required to redress inequity, so conservatism relies on ethics.
7 How ethical are people, particularly people with power? Can they be trusted to do what is right in accordance with popular ideology?

Footnotes

[1] G. West Chruchman, *Challenge to Reason,* McGraw-Hill, 1968, Chapters I and II.
[2] H. A. Simon, *Models of Man: Social and Rational,* Wiley, 1957.
[3] O. H. Taylor, *A History of Economics Thought,* McGraw-Hill, 1960, Chapter 17.
[4] J. K. Galbraith, *The Affluent Society,* Houghton Mifflin, 1960, Chapter XIII.
[5] P. Starr, *Social Transformation of American Medicine,* Basic Books, 1982, p. 148 Lassim.

[6] C. A. Reich, *Greening of America,* Bantam, 1970, p. 333.
[7] see R.P. Wolf, *Understanding Rawls,* Princeton, 1977, especially Part I.
[8] see Robert W. Poole, Jr., (Ed), *Instead of Regulation,* Lexington, 1982. The essays in this volume tend to suggest reliance on the market rather than regulation works. However, one looks in vain for any but a market motive.
[9] G. Gilder, *Spirit of Enterprice,* Simon & Schuster, 1984.
[10] L. Thurow, *Generating Inequality,* Basu Books, 1975.

Part I

Chapter II
Are Justice, Fairness and Ethics Real?

1 Perceptions and Conceptions

According to some ancient Greek ideals the goals of a philosophically ideal society should be truth, goodness and beauty. We generally accept them as our own, if we think about such things. But such idealized goals are utopian and need definition. We may speculate about them knowing all the while they are always beyond a distant horizon. To practical people, however, more understandable goals as happiness, income, health, power, and other mundane, more or less attainable ends, become ready substitutes for the far off, ethereal ends of activity.

The means to the far off or to the attainable goals are themselves severely limited by other values even after agreement on definition is reached. There is a triad of values which, however, we should like to believe constrain all private and public actions. They are Justice, Fairness and Ethics.

The definitions of these value conceptions which are both means and ends are not universally agreed upon. The essence of a useful definition is that it describes an idea or a thing so that it is generally recognizable and usable. We can define and describe what does not exist, say a unicorn. Unicorns do not exist so far as most of us are concerned. At least no person has seen a unicorn in the flesh. The detailed attributes of a unicorn, then, exist only in the minds of story tellers and artists who have described them. Communications on the subject of unicorns, their food and care, are not operational, although unicorns may have a large following of believers.

Now any definition is absolute in the sense that unicorns are definitionally absolute according to which artist or story teller one follows. Horses are absolute by definition just as unicorns are, but the characteristics of horses can be examined because they exist outside someone's mind as well as in it. Horses, as perceptions, can be discussed in a different way from unicorn discussions.[1]

Justice, fariness and ethics are somewhere between horses and unicorns. They are absolute by definition, and they also have alternative definitions. They are qualities with characteristics which we believe we perceive, and which we talk about with some degree of meaning. They are operational as well as purely conceptual. One can evoke fairness in behavior but one cannot produce a unicorn to prove a point.

A man receives $10 for doing some task. Is it a just wage? A fair one? The early Christian theologians were bemused by such questions. Just wages and prices, and the idea of fair exchange worried the Church Fathers, just as did questions of the fairness and justice of slavery. Later economists, although assuring the world at large that their discipline was value free and thoroughly objective, developed a theory, a fairly reasonable one, of income distribution. The theory is so constrained by assumptions that the theoretical findings have little direct relation to reality. But the findings do suggest that in an ideal, theoretical, not necessarily moral, world, each factor is paid according to its contribution to the final product.

This marginal productivity analysis quickly became a moral legitimation for market behavior because it was held to be just. Each factor earned what it produced, hence to what it was entitled (by moral law?). The refined assumptions were, for the time, justified by the assertion that each factor *tended* to receive its fair share, fair or just in terms of its contribution. Therefore the moral course to be followed, as a public policy was to assure the reality of the assumptions – pure and perfect competition! Reality, what the economists started out to analyze, became a hindrance to justice! One may assert with equal ease and credulity that the assumptions provide a model or system which is a distorted picture of reality.[2] This however does not negate the tendencies of the model, including the tendency for justice, to be accomplished by equating income to productive contribution.

Fairness and justice are important forces. Both legitimate behavior, including market behavior, and when defined in an acceptable fashion, affect activity and make it functional. That is to say the market works better, and with less dissension, when it is conceived to be just and fair. Markets are institutions not natural phenomena.

2 Some Definitions

With all this in mind we shall undertake definitions of just and fair. Such definitions apply to the current discussion. For other purposes or for other analyses other definitions may be devised. A diamond is a girl's best friend for some purposes, but a diamond also is a token of engagement or a symbol of great hardness. If our definitions are useful in explaining and understanding market behavior we may assert they have the operationality which is essential in any analysis.

We define (for the market and market economy) justice as the condition in which a person is rewarded in accordance with his or her contribution to the final product. Legitimated ownership of capital is also a claim for the marginal product of capital. But justice is only an approximation because it is beyond our knowledge to estimate exactly, or in some instances even very closely, the value of a factoral input. Accounting does not tell us exactly the contribution of a person or a machine to the final value of a product. Accounting gives us an approximation. Justice then is not *exactly* done by the market process of income distribution or imputation.

Fairness, by our definition, is treating a person (or factor) similarly to the way similarly situated and endowed persons (or factors) are treated in the market. Women and men should, as a matter of fairness, receive the same or similar rewards for identical or similar productive accomplishment according to this conception. The question of fairness becomes sticky if we extend the idea to the rewards for comparable work. What does comparable mean? How does one compare a truckdriver with a stenographer? The techniques of grading and ranking jobs are not so scientifically and logically sound as one should like. Job evaluation and classification in industry have had a pragmatic acceptance which may or may not justify their extension generally.

Fairness, in a sense, not only equalizes differences, it also combats envy. Where envy arises out of the (covert) perception that similar economic efforts are better or worse rewarded, fairness equalizes the rewards and so reduces envy. Envy which is based upon incorrect perceptions of why rewards are unequal is a malignant social ill.

Ultimately justice and fairness are estimated by the exercise of judgment. Justice and fairness are allied, but they also conflict. They are the scales on which law and behavior are weighed.

Ethics we define as a freely willed action by a person, the action expressing the *value* system of the person at the time and place of the action. A personal value system is a reflection, sometimes out of focus, of the person's perception of a widely held social ethic, in a given circumstance. The role of judgment in ethical matters is evident. Terrorists, as well as more ordinary people believe they are doing good in the light of some legitimated goal. Ethical considerations include both beneficial and harmful effects. Unethics is a special case of ethics.

While fairness and justice are really part of the ongoingness of the functioning market, an ethical act is *outside* the market and its rules. It is a freely willed expression to do good (or evil). Justice and fairness are ongoing functions *in* the market. Ethical legitimation is rarely resorted to, and when employed often becomes part of the market baggage and so becomes part of justice and fairness in the ensuing periods. An ethical act is classified by one's perception of some set of social values.

Why should anyone in the market place be concerned with ethics? Stated another way "Of what use is ethics to the society, or to me? Some one who is the recipient of my generous act may be better off, but so what? Is the society better off? Am I better off?"

Such questions view ethics, in or out of the market context, as instrumental. When the American genius Ben Franklin declared that "Honesty is the best policy," he made a statement which allows many interpretations and hence alternative meanings. Honesty may be viewed as:

1 essential to business success (personal instrumentalism)
2 essential to successful market organization (macro instrumentalism)
3 essential to the "good life" for the person involved (personal happiness, without regard to business success)
4 essential to social well being (macro harmony without reference to income maximization)
5 pleasing to God or some other superior entity (deontological).

The last possible meaning approaches the religious and so, valid as it might be, is generally irrelevant to the present restricted, secular market oriented discussion.

The first two possible meanings are clearly instrumental. The self interest of the business manager or of the market organization is better served if managers act honestly than if they do not. Honesty in this sense is not a value independent of the market requirements. It is, in effect, a requirement of business policy since it leads to success.

Honesty then is comparable to a computer or advertising program. If one wants to succeed in business, or if the market is to function efficiently then honesty should be the managerial rule. It is in this sense that Ben Franklin's advice is usually taken. Honesty produces a yield in excess of its cost, thus honesty is, on the net, profitable.

But the next two possible interpretations really go beyond market measures. They assert that the manager and presumably his firm, and the society somehow benefit or at least are affected in ways which cannot be measured by money or goods if honesty is the rule. How to prove this is not clear nor is a general proof likely. We all know people who, now and again, play fast and loose with honesty in the market and seem to do very well and have the appearance of being happy. We all know of social critics who can prove that any social and economic system in existence or in imagination is either doomed to some form of dishonesty and social disharmony. Capitalism, socialism, politics, the family, art, and so on all come in for criticisms which prove that each is a fraud or worse. Every conceivable system has its critics. Even Heaven had Lucifer. So at the social level the legitimation of honesty may sometimes be questioned and is questionable.

3 The Use of Ethics

Now let us revert to market ethics and the questions which we imagined some realistic cynic to pose. "Why do we need an ethic?" Or do we need a market ethic?" Our answer goes to the meaningfulness of the questions. We need to reflect on business ethics because we cannot avoid having *some* ethical content in the structure of a market. Choices are available to us, but not the choice of no ethics at all. Ethics is implicit in both individual and social behavior. We do not have eyes in order to see, or hands in order to grasp. We see *because* we have eyes, we grasp because we have hands. Ethics is like hands or eyes, and is an implicit element in social behavior. Ethics are roughly analogous to our bodily construction. Both body and an ethic simply are! This is a central theme of this discussion. Human behavior implies some set of values.

Action in a social world, or in more refined focus, personal action in the world of markets and business reflects, in some fashion, the values of the greater society. And the values of the greater society reflect, often in a confused fashion, the various values of individuals and groups of the past and present. Laws, customs, conventions of behavior contain and exhibit values which are found in the society. And man is, among other things, a social animal. Individuals are bathed in the values of society.[3] Some values are thoughtlessly followed, some internalized almost as unconscious springs of future behavior, some social values are rejected out of hand, some after reflection or after trying them out. But even the most rational, hard headed businessman who is totally dedicated to efficiency and his own fortune, nevertheless accepts efficiency and his own fortune as worthy goals. He is operating in accordance with an ethic. Criticism, social and private, may be directed at this profit maximizing, unsocial being, but the more telling critical slings and arrows are directed against an ethic, an ideology, a value in action. E.F. Hutton's check writing operation, exposed in 1985, was not criticized because it was successful and saved the Company money. It was criticized because it cheated small banks of the interest on over $1 billion, which incidentally many banks did not know they were entitled to.

Our profit making, rational automaton (called the economic man) may disregard what we in our wisdom consider an acceptable viewpoint and ethic. We may even try to argue and reason with the successful automaton. But there will be no compromise or conversion until and unless we can persuade him that his approach to rational behavior is essentially irrational because the market and the society will destroy, or at least restrict, him unless he becomes more sensitive to the needs and ideologies of others. The appeal is self interest. "Unless you stop what you are doing, and change your style of behavior, you are doomed." Such a warning may work. The market and the society have the capacity to enforce the threat. But the exercise is neither one of ethics nor logic. It is strictly one of power, persuasion and self interest. It is a social sanction.

One of the preconceptions of this discussion, and ensuing discussions is that there is no coherent, universally accepted value system. There is, however, an interactive set of values, some vague, some rigid, some antithetical to each other, some competing. The set or definable, tolerably self contained parts are sufficiently coherent to be considered ideologies. We use the plural because some of the partial values hang together and are accepted, in a persistent way, by some groups in society, while other collections of values are appealing to other groups. In short, opinions, varying values, social and private are held by different people. Each person is neither his own prophet nor philosopher. There are schools of philosophers and cults of prophets, in a metaphorical sense. There are also ideological conflicts e.g. over abortion or granting federal tax credits for state and local taxes. Many ideological conflicts however do not create significant social conflict e.g. issues of the sharing of household duties, or incorporating or not incorporating a professional activity.

Values as well as technologies change. We do not believe there is a single course or instigator of change. There are interactions among all facets of the society, several facets being associations of people with more or less shared values. Blacks, Hispanics, the Women's Movement, Right to Lifers, Environmentalists are examples of minority, often single purpose associations. But older, more multi-functional groups also exist, often treated as "The Establishment". Business and trade associations as well as informal groups of business people are joined by ideological forces. Labor is similarly formally and informally associated. Smaller groups e.g. steelmakers or auto mechanics may share values, *inter sese*.

The values or ideologies originate in diverse ways. There is no generally accepted theory of value structure. Historical values such as a free press persist, even though the applications of the traditional rules seem bizarre to many who support the values. Pornography in magazines and movies which violates other values, does not seem to all free press supporters, to warrant First Amendment protection. Similarly restrictions on mergers or other market behaviors which to some are protective of the ancient value of market structure, to others seem in violation of equally ancient values of performance. The flow of values may be from the general society to the specific activity i.e. the market, or the reverse. The values may also have origins in apparently unfunctionally related social undertakings. World War II attracted women and Blacks into industry. After the war the expectations of these groups, as well as the accepted values of other groups e.g. trade unions, employers, government administrators and parts of the public at large, accepted the new arrangements as proper and legitimate. The propaganda of the Four Freedoms of World War II became ingredients of policy after the war. Market structure was surely affected by the acceptance of public policies toward employment, and health and public administration was affected by the ideas of social protection.

Such changes in ideology are also changes in the private and public expectations of the institutions in question. In general, with respect to business as an institution, one may suggest that the business is expected, as a matter of popular faith, to act "properly". In the 1950s and 1960s business and the public often expressed the view that business should "act responsibly" and to "be a good citizen". In other words behavior beyond mere market behavior was an ideal widely held. This is not the same as Milton Friedman's ideas of the business of business being business, or even Cal Coolidge's aphorism that the business of America is America's business.

As times became less good in the late 1960s, as unemployment and inflation were feared, as evidence of less than ideal behavior by business was revealed in the Nixon and post Nixon administrations public attitudes toward business changed as did business self perceptions. The behavior expected of business became more ordered. Social responsibility as an active force was, to a degree, supplanted by the belief that business should not be *irresponsible* with respect to the environment, honesty, quality and human dignity. Business, for its part, became more active in politics, especially in financing politicians through Political Action Committees, and more defensive of business as an institution.

The motive power for such changes did not originate in technology or markets but in the several forces, including technology and market structure, which propel society. Social interacton, the emergence of particular problems e.g. OPEC, the armaments race, and the influence of particular personalities, these and a myriad of issues, problems, social forces, technological changes, and habits of thought and so on endlessly molded and changed ideologies and behavior. Cause, in social situations, is almost always multiple. There is, so far as we can see, no set, fixed hierarchy of causes which foment social change.

So ethical behavior may have an element of self interest in it. But this should come as no surprise. Motives of people, both in individual action and in group action, as by a managerial group, are almost always mixed. If self interest and the public interest coincide, everyone benefits. It is where the public or *some* private interest oppose some other private interest that the ethical issues become apparent. It is not improbable that the conservative social reaction to the public concern with civil rights, to birth control of various sorts, against the Vietnam disaster and government regulation, and to other such non market phenomena somehow linked up with the business ideology of the desirability of efficiency, even at some social cost. Under Reagan regulation was out. The resulting socio-economic conservatism did not mesh comfortably with the individualistic *cum* regulation ideological mix which spanned the 1920s to the 1960s in America. Ideology is rarely if ever seamless and unique. Regulation in some form probably will reappear.

In our conception ethical action, like social and private actions realistically may have a mix of self interest and unselfish motive. But what distinguishes ethical behavior from other kinds of behavior is that the self interest component in ethical action is usually less than in other kinds of behavior. The self interest of the manager in promoting a subordinate to a higher job, or buying from A rather than B, is presumably motivated and guided by ideas and ideals of efficiency, which is to say self interest. But choosing to distribute the charitable gifts of a firm in a given pattern reflects both the self interest of manager and firm, as well as the belief that the fit will be more likely to satisfy the idea of "goodness" if given to one beneficiary rather than another. If this disinterested element is lacking, the gift is more like an advertising expenditure than a gift. In a social sense, support of a pro or anti policy with respect to abortion or anti trust or regional development is rarely based solely or even mainly on self interest.

Thus we conclude that in our conception ethical behavior by the firm via the manager is behavior of a generous nature, with generosity being of greater significance than in non ethical or less ethical undertakings. The question is not to have or not to have an ethic in business. The realistic question is what ethic to embrace.

4 Ethics of the Market

The ensuing discussions will attempt to throw some light on the way market or business ethics are structured and delimited. The interconnectedness between social and private values is the major theme.

From our standpoint, an ethical course of market behavior should be one (1) which is freely chosen from among alternatives, (2) which includes both a moral and technical dimension, (3) and in which the actor compares (a) what he believes is morally acceptable on the social level and (b) what he believes his course of action should be. These are the elements necessary to set up a moral tension in the actor. The release of that tension by some action or inaction constitutes for him the moral decision.

The ethical act by the actor is chosen from more than one possible course of behavior. There is thus an evaluation which implies a criticism among the alternatives and their implications. Such criticism by the actor (the manager of the firm) is part and parcel of the decision process, and is not generally publicly desclosed. Ethical behavior is like artistic behavior in that it is a criticism of the observed world. The artist no less than the ethicist rearranges the world. However the *observer,* too, either the disinterested commentator or the interested court, administrator or other involved person, also makes evaluative judgments and criticisms.

Such observers can never really know what went on in the mind of the manager. His choice process is also probably a mystery to him, although he may be prepared to defend it by logic, experience and rule. The socially relevent discussion largely occurs among those who did not contribute directly to the decision (they are making the social statement of "what was expected"). This statement is a *post hoc* comment on what the *ante hoc* values were or should have been. The rationalization or justification of the decision maker becomes part of the *post hoc* comment in the sense that it expresses the actor's conception of his responsibility to the social scene.

The social comment made by individuals are of extreme importance in legitimating or refusing to legitimate some managerial action. If the legitimation is widely accepted it becomes part of the social convention. If the legitimation is by a court, it may become part of the precedent which plays a role in determining future court decisions. The court in a real sense is the observing critic testing, by critieria of precedent, interpretation of the facts in the light of the court's rendering of the law. There is added the court's conception of justice and ethics. This conception again grows out of the tension between the court's apperceptions, which are personal, and its perceptions, which it believes to be an objective evaluation of "what is expected" in the situation.

The market for practical purposes is structured by considerations of efficiency and amenity, or more precisely by efficiency and law.[4] Efficiency reflects the managerial perceptions of appropriate technology and business organization. The manager of each undertaking makes the necessary choices. In this he or she is guided by the motives of business managers toward success, profits, perpetuity of values, sales, share of market, etc.

The law or amenity forces derive from social values as well as from considerations which the society generates, after compromises in the legislature and in less formal social experiences and considerations. Law, administrative rule and regulation tend to limit, for example, the uses of technology e.g. hazardous chemicals, as well as to restrain certain organizational forms e.g. monopoly. These are amenity restrictions on the market, and so are part of market structure.

The third element in the market structuring after efficiency and law is, of course, prices, money or any other means of payment. The monetary force is really an allocative device which is used to attract and put labor, capital and technology in place, and to measure success and failure.

5 Order and Change

An earlier generation of ecomomists and statisticians was fascinated by business cycles and cycle theory. Order was sought in a flow of events which seemed to deny order. With Keynes and the prosperous aftermath of World War II came a lessening of interest in business cycles and one may add, income distribution theory. The analytical interest shifted to order and orderliness of production (linear progamming) and growth. Yet in economic life, in the political and social world, reforms and market interventions persist as marks of all societies. They are components of progress. Such interventionistic policy on both national and international levels seemed to assume that ethical considerations and ethical structure were either considered not worthy of much debate or were assumed to be well known and operative. The assumption was that efficiency, i.e. more production, which of course depended on some production and management theories, was the major objective of the economy. Yet at this time the market interventions included enormous income transfers and "entitlements" to those who presumably needed help because of low income. It was as if an effective, productive society assuaged feelings of guilt because some sectors had income which decency considered insufficient. This was the era of great interest in development theory.

Yet a general theory of income transfers and their effects, social and economic, was only partly developed, possibly because the idea of income transfers and entitlements as a social ideal and ethical assumption did not tie the economic fraternity together, and did not have support of any well structured groups in the business, political or social worlds. Income transfers had not become internalized as had the ideas of free public schools, public health and anti trust. In the generally prosperous post W.W. II years economists were more concerned with technical economies than with devising a theory for the setting of markets. The social environment was given short shrift by economic theory and economists at precisely the time when environmental and ideological changes were rampant. That markets are an aspect of society in its broad sense was, of course, known. However economics become a discipline of mathematics, statistics, model building and small problems. Technique overshadowed relevance.

The election of Reagan in 1980 and the conservative control of the U.S. national legislature led to a limitation of the income transfer policy and the entitlement idea. The attack on these ethical principles, however forced a concentration of counter social, political and economic ideologies and forces into a more unified stance. Prior to the 1984 general elections the

Democratic Party, the political center of the income transfer and market intervention, began its ideological reformation. It is interesting to note that conservatism along with social liberalism always had some place in the Democratic Party. Moderate Republicans also were at odds with Republican Conservatism. On the net, American Conservatism probably suffered in the presidential election of 1988 in which Bush was the victor.

In our view the current social ethic often used to evaluate market activity is to consider the negative externalities of business behavior. When the society was, in general more prosperous and ruly, say after World War II until the 1960s, the major social ideal applied to business was that it be "responsible". That is to say business was seen by itself, and often in the public perception, as producing goods and jobs as a norm. As a kind of bonus, business was also to be a "good citizen" and exhibit "responsibility". It is as if extra benefits were expected of business by its enthusiastic spokespersons as well as by politicians and others in the public sector. Just what was implied is not at all clear, but a feeling of social success was in the air.

When, however, the Watergate scandal erupted and the post Watergate scandals (1971–74) of business behavior become known, when individualism on the American and Western European scene exploded into hippies and flower children, and when adults followed the social lead of children, when the rights of minorities, women, and other splinter or disadvantaged groups became major social issues, then the public expectations of what business should provide changed. This was also the period when the ideal of "system" as a useful way to look at social and other phenomena became popular. In technology all sorts of servomechanisms based on feedback became widely used. Related was the great public awareness and market use of electronic calculators, computers, and robotics. The way of looking at events shifted from an event being a unique happening, to an event being part of a larger, interactive unity. Unemployment of Blacks, for example, was not so much a statistic as a part of a bigger economic scene. Once, Blacks, then called Negroes, were often simply not part of the market system. Now Blacks are the unemployed and *victims* of the system. So with smoke – once it was a material which would simply disappear in the vast sea of air. Now it is poison or worse, floating in the environment with serious ecological significance. Examples of the systemic way of looking at events could easily be multiplied.

The result of all this is to make people more sensitive to the significance of what once were isolated and small events. Isolated events led to first discovering the host of anti-social infractions which occur in the real world, and then to implementing organizations of various sorts to stop or correct the infractions. Women's and minority rights, ecological safety, armament limitation, health and safety protection and so on, endlessly, became the social expectation of business as well as government and general private and public responsibility. President Johnson, with his populist leanings and support, pushed the movement in the U.S. President Carter, however, half tried to stem it and was defeated by Reagan who vigorously embraced a conservative market efficiency ideology.Ideologically, reform was tired.

Reagan became President of the U.S. on a program, generally speaking of "get government off our backs," i.e. reduce government amenity intervention. He did not succeed although he probably has planted seeds which will grow into an ideology of efficiency in the management of government. It is an undecided issue whether, in the long view, the U.S., and indeed the Western World will give up, easily or not, the systemic view of the events of the world, and the love affair with social amenities.

Politicians, public administrators, lawyers and judges, as well as more ordinary people expect certain kinds of patterns of behavior of each other and of the society in general. These expectations are part of ideology. Rarely if ever is ideology entirely homogeneous among people of the same society. Value conflicts and disagreements over means, when ends are generally accepted, are normal in a society, especially one so free as is the United States. What is true for the society also applies to the detail of market behavior.

6 The Perception of Market Ethics

The ethical content of behavior, social and personal, is an important element in legitimating the behavior. In recent years the business society seems to have become more self conscious of its social role than in the past. Traditionally the rising standard of living, the easing of the burdens of labor, the rising of expectations which often were met and in a decade or less surpassed, made business the model of a successful social undertaking. To be sure more and more was wanted, to be sure business was criticized as heartless, as materialistic, as not doing enough, and so on from the left as well as from other business critics. Such criticism was by a social minority. By and large, business was self confident, even self congratulatory. If only the critics understood, they would be quiet. Knowledge was the key to the appreciation of business. But in the past decade or so, business has begun to look inward, to itself, to ascertain whether or not it can legitimate itself.

The moral and ethical basis of any society, ours among them, is complex. What society has done over time is often to reduce personally held and publicly debated ethical values – ideology (i.e. values in action) into rules, conventions and laws. These affect the structure of markets and the values and behavior of business managers. Rules replace what once were personally held values. A persistent view of business is that it gets things done, and is therefore effective. To be businesslike is a compliment. But those who daily live with business or its study know that to be entirely businesslike can never be totally realized even by the most efficient business.

Business operates in markets and markets, at first glance, are organized as efficiency instruments. Inputs per unit of output are to be minimized or outputs per unit of input to be maximized. If there is an ethical basis for economic theory or what may be called "text book economics", it is this minimization-maximization ideal. But markets are not guided *only* by ideas of efficiency. Amenity is real and is intrinsic. In the political market some ideal of peace as non war and non violence is held superior to mutual destruction. In the economic market self interest is the motive as the Father of Political Economy so effectively taught. But Adam Smith did recognize "sympathy"; (we should say empathy) as a natural characteristic of people which limited self interest in the market. Friedman would have "charity" always outside the market. But markets and people in reality are not organized so that efficiency is the sole motive. The inefficiencies may be due to ignorance or structural market obstacles, which economists seem to accept, or to Smith's "sympathy" as expounded on his *Theory of Moral Sentiments*.

Does reliance on the efficiency tend toward the best economic society? The answer of "pure" theory is "yes," if the good is defined as the largest net total income. (But the logic is not certain nor are all the relevant conditions included.) It is fairly clear that the maxims of ethics which are generally accepted in our world are not limited to the macro income's size. Its distribution and the terms and conditions of its generation are also important, maybe of more importance in some circumstances, than sheer size of income. The terms and conditions of income generation and its distribution, as well as its size, are issues requiring "active duty" in Smith's words. He asserts in his *Theory of Moral Sentiments* that "The most sublime speculation of the contemplative philosopher can scarce compensate the neglect of the smallest active duty".

The characteristics of the market, realistically viewed, are efficiency *and* amenity. The former is a technical or technological ideal, the latter a humane or humanistic ideal, which may be reductive of efficiency. Together they structure the market, that is regulate or control individual behavior. Amenity is not only introduced by social and legislative forces e.g. minimum wages, maximum hours, ecological considerations, quality controls, etc.; amenity is also introduced by personal choice of managers e.g. considerations of health and safety independent of or prior to legislation, educational provision for employees and their families, quality control etc. The degree to which the individual introduction of amenity is independent of any efficiency consideration is impossible to tell. Do the managers of, say, large U.S. corporations buy time on Public Television because it is a cheap way to advertise, or are there other more subtle motives? Are the child care facilities of many European factories motivated *only* by efficiency considerations, or are there more noble motives?

To delegate managerial authority to managers is to give them, within ill defined limits, the power to direct the energies of the enterprise as they, the managers, think appropriate. Justice, fairness and ethics are all part of the choice process. Lacking any legal impropriety, owners can only correct managerial behavior by persuasion or by removing the managers. But often the apparent non efficiency actions of managers win the approval of owners, or a large fraction of ownership, because such behavior is in accord with the ideological values of the owners as well as because the behavior is believed somehow to enhance efficiency. The ideological acceptance of doing good (albeit within limits) and of securing efficiencies of production and sale cannot be separated in an ongoing business.

What ultimately justifies legitimate managerial behavior is success. Did the enterprise do well i.e. earn a reasonable profit, win a large enough share of the market, grow, avoid difficulties with and enjoy the approbation of labor, government and the public? The balancing of efficiency considerations and amenity considerations in the act of responsible behavior obviously includes the control over technical know how and acceptable values.

7 Inefficiencies as Implicit

This discussion is directed at the amenity idea as it flows from managerial behavior. Of greater practical significance, however, is the *restriction* on managerial behavior imposed by law and convention or customary expectation. The law and convention as forces structuring markets represent a kind of social consensus, often crude and ill thought through, but sometime exquisitely subtle, approving, disapproving, requiring or forbidding certain kinds of actions. Pure food and drug requirements, insider trading, building codes, or bank reserve requirements each represent a social value which has been written into law and regulation. Often the rules and regulations are too general by themselves to be applied. All who read may not read correctly. Then, someone, the managers, courts or other administrative agencies have to apply or interpret the rules.

Whether the rules are interpreted by a manager or ultimately by a court of law, it is fairly clear that responsibility, provided both in moral or ideologic values and in technical know-how, are present. Their application and interpretation might be, violative of amenity and frustrating of efficiency. This, I take it, is a prime criticism by political and economic conservatives of liberal legislation.[7]

Efficiency may be measured by some absolute criteria; amenity cannot. The latter is a social intention. It is a value ideal but one which, without some technical basis and constraint to legitimate it, might become an overwhelming burden both to those it was created to help and to everyone else affected. Tariffs, wage fixing, social insurance, ecological legislation, and so on all have, at various times, been charged with being socially dysfunctional. Yet the folk wisdom or artful persuasion tend to insist upon restrictions on the market as being in accord with some social ideals or needs.

In the U.S. there is the judicial distinction between *per se* and the rule of reason. A *per se* action is improper, illegal and prohibited regardless of any positive values it might generate. Conspiracy to hurt someone, for example, cannot be permitted even if the net results would be *generally* beneficial. It simply is beyond the law. On the other hand other actions having to do, say, with mergers and acquisitions or share of markets or the spending of enterprise funds on seemingly nonproductive ways *may* be appropriate. The court would examine the reasonableness i.e. the responsible nature of the action and then rule in the light of reason.

Statute law with clear-cut requirements and prohibitions may tend to restrict the application of the rule of reason. Common law and statute law which indicate only the direction and nature of public policy invites courts and administravite bodies to rely on the rule of reason. In such cases, it is obvious that the ideology, background, values, knowledge and sense of responsibility of the judges and public administrators become significant inputs to the final decision. But courts and administrators are also restrained by their sense of the fitness of things, of what is expected of them in the light of custom, tradition and respect for value continuity. Hence responsibility of managers, judges and administrators cannot be taken for granted. There is always a risk in reason just as there is a risk in rigid requirement.

Footnotes

[1] C. L. Lastrucci *The Scientific Approach* p 114 ff. Schenkman, 1967.
[2] Ibid.
[3] H. A. Sumong "Rational Decision Making in Business Organization". American Economic Reveiw, Sept. 1979.
[4] W. G. Sheperd. *The Economics of Industrial Organization* p 226 ff. Prentice Hall 1979.
[5] S. C. Sufrin and J. E. Owers. "The Ethics of Anti Trust". *International Reviev of Economics and Business* n. 4–5 April–May 1988.

Chapter III
A Canon of Ethics

1 Complexity of Market Ethics

The issues of ethics may be divided into process and structure. How one makes an ethical decision is as interesting and stimulating both intellectually and morally as the decision made.

In 1916 Henry Ford, the elder, determined to reduce the dividends paid the shareholders so as to "spread the benefits of this industrial system to the greatest possible number, to help them (i.e. employees) build up their lives and their homes".[1] The company was almost a family corporation. Ford meant to increase employment by a vertical expansion of the company's operations, and raise wages. Minority stockholders sued, arguing (à la Friedman) that the company's purpose was their profits. Ford later bought them out.

In 1963, after the calamitous bombing of a black Birmingham church, in which 4 young children were killed, Roger Blough, President of U.S. Steel, a very large local employer, said "for a corporation to attempt to exert any kind of economic compulsion to achieve a particular end in the racial area seems to me quite beyond what a corporation should do".[8]

In the two preceding paragraphs we have different views as to the appropriate behavior of large business firms. Ford, as the lawsuit indicated, was interested in "taking care" of his employees (later criticized as paternalism). Blough, on the other hand, doubted the morality of using the power of the firm to impose a value on a community, even if the value had social legitimation.

The goals of both Ford and Blough undoubtedly included the financial and business success of their respective companies. The goals clearly, however, were more than short run profits for shareholders. Both men had a long view of the firm, as is borne out by other statements and policies. But Ford included as a goal his vision of employee well being. This view was not shared by some stockholders and by critics who feared that the

Ford policy might or would reduce the choices and unduly influence the behavior of employees. Paternalism, as a general rule, is not socially legitimate in the American ideology. High wages, generally speaking, are.

Blough wanted to distance himself and his company from non plant racial matters. His denial that the firm as a "good citizen" (to use his words) should do anything about racial violence did not carry over to his firm's not doing anything about congressional or national elections, or lobbying for public policy beneficial to U.S. Steel. U.S. Steel was not utterly divorced from questions of national public policy. The means used by Ford or Blough, or of the Ford Motor Company and U.S. Steel, to gain their complex of social goals are obviously related to the goals sought.

Until and unless the goal to be achieved by a moral act or ethical judgment is known, the ethical exercise is incomplete. When the goal or purpose is known, then a technical evaluation of means and implications can be made. Honesty, for example, may be the best policy to (a) sell more shoes, to (b) win more friends, to (c) make one feel good, or to (d) attain nobility of spirit. It is obvious that the maximization of (a) or (b) or (c) or (d) has costs. To maximize (a) may be to reduce any or all of the other possible goals below each one's maximum. If (a) to (d) are all considered as part of income, psychic or otherwise, it is clear that maximizing any goal implies an opportunity cost in that the other desired goals will be less than a maximum. *Ethical goals, which are generally viewed as of great value, personal and public, cannot be achieved without cost.* It is surprising that so many people in the business world expect the kudos and respect stemming from the public recognition of their ethical worth to be a concomitant without any cost to business success. Good works require income and wealth to carry them out. But ethical behavior within business and within the market may not be for all to see and judge. Public awareness of good works is not automatic.

2 Morality is Personal

Since the undertaking of an ethical act is personal, even private, we must look for some personal or private way for a person to consider the ethics or morality of his or her action. An action can be judged by its consequences or implications. The purpose of rain is not to water plants. Rain has no purpose, it is a natural necessity. Irrigation systems *are* instituted to water plants. That is their purpose.

A social action tends to be purposive. An action is consciously undertaken and events follow. The benefits and the hurts may be separately aggregated, and some measure of the degree of net benefit or hurt assessed. Business builds a factory to make goods. The factory is the means, goods the purpose. However people not connected with the business may be benefitted or hurt by the building operation. Such results may be without reference to the purpose or goal of the action. Purpose and goal are subjectively determined, in our sense.

Ethics, however, is nothing if it is not a free will, purposive undertaking. The (self conscious) ethical actor should attempt to estimate the results, market and non market, of an undertaking. In other words, for an ethical act the implications should be, insofar as possible, determined *before* the action. The action first is imagined and evaluated. Thus thoughtfulness, self consciousness, analysis, experience and of course hunch become part of the ethical enterprise. Only then is action undertaken.

In a grand sense the utilitarian greatest good for the greatest number comes to mind as a major altruistic aphorism. Sadly, in our opinion, Bentham's "greatest good" is only a vague and not very effective guide. That ethical behavior is behavior which "does good" either positively or by alleviating hurt or bad behavior is, we may suppose, generally agreed on. But the greatest good for the greatest number inevitably drags us into the morass of trying to measure a large number of non comparable effects on an extremely large number of people. Useful generalizations are usually limited in scope.

We recognize that for practical purposes we can compare or otherwise evaluate some amenities or useful services in a public or social way, although many amenities and services are difficult to compare. For example drinking water free of harmful and noisome additions is generally accepted as a social good. A person who would undertake to supply such water to a community with no benefits accruing to him but thanks and praise, would be an ethical benefactor. But suppose a high minded person undertook to supply food to the hungry. The food he provided was ham sandwiches while the impoverished planned beneficiaries were Orthodox Jews or Moslems. The action would scarcely have been effective. Even though the motive was praiseworthy the action would have been a failure. If, however, one philanthropist supplied needed water to a parched society, and another supplied food to a hungry society, a comparison of the virtue of each would be beside the point and impossible. Both would elicit ethical praise. And praise, not price is a payment for such behavior.

But even where there is a widepread social agreement as to the acknowledged goodness of an act, doing good for the whole world, or for a million people is a different undertaking than doing good for a dozen people or for a defined group. For were the richest person in the world to share equally all her wealth with all the poor in the world, or even of the nation or city, the spread of benefits would be so thin as to be meaningless. Yet the same money and effort concentrated on a more closely defined group or on a single project might have spectacular benefits. The full scholarships to relatively few students may be more educationally effective than an equal expenditure of money and effort to a whole generation of students, each one receiving a pittance. The greatest good to the greatest number is less a guide to ethical behavior than it is a hint that good should not, as a *general matter* be concentrated in a particular, arbitrary defined class or group.[3] It is a class correction.

What the utilitarians have given ethical theory is the idea that morality is not a solitary absolute but rather part of the social fabric. It can be part of politics, business, education, part of any social undertaking, and its legitimation is social and personal, its outreach narrow or wide. What utilitarianism cannot provide, and, so far as we can see, nor can any other ethical system either, is a list of directives and inhibitions to behavior.[4] Even the Golden Rule and the Categorical Imperative miss the diverse nature of what different people consider as good and desirable, and the enormous ignorance as to alternative means to accomplish ethical ends. Unless means and ends are known, ethical behavior is risky. Unless the distribution of welfare as well as the size of welfare are known, knowledge of any welfare exercise is incomplete.

From our viewpoint the tendency for religions to codify certain ethical norms or rules of behavior is a common trait. "Thou shalt not kill" is, we are most likely to grant, a reasonable rule whose implications go far beyond the pragmatic. (Soldiers in battle are generally excluded.) Not killing or not making a practice of killing, aside from its obvious social consequences, has other implications. It circumscribes the power functions of the individual, thus expanding the power potential of government; it suggests a guilt result if one disobeys the Commandment.

The avoidance of guilt becomes a phenomenon of relieving a potential tension between the social value-people should not kill each other, *as a social rule,* and for the personal value of not killing. In most societies, although there are exceptions, speaking generally, social harmony is abetted by not sanctioning murder. Even people who hunt wild game sometimes exhibit feelings of guilty uneasiness at hunting deer or other large game. This reaction is probably a socially learned attitude. I never have heard of a fisherman expressing any deep regret or guilt at having caught a fish, or even a hunter for having shot down a duck or goose. Regret for killing deer or other large animals is frequent. It is as if there are residual reasons for feeling uneasy at killing some living beings other than humans.

With respect to humans, there may be departures from the inhibition on killing:

1 The military justification
2 The exercise of legal penalties by some governments
3 Extraordinary personal circumstances as in self protection or the protection of another person.

3 Reasonable Behavior and Automatic Restraints

But murder is not a usual occurance in our universe of discourse. In the more parochial and prosaic setting of the marketplace there also are rules and shibboleths. That conspiracy among buyers and sellers is improper is recognized by law and custom. In the U.S. the Anti Trust laws were enacted and later interpreted as results of social pressures. But social pressures for particular interpretations were not always unanimous. The laws themselves are often compromises, and the decisions under the laws were not always unanimous, nor totally supported by the involved and aware parties. Conspiracy in the form of price fixing remains moderately common in the U.S. if the number of suits entered into by the government against price fixing is an index. Not a week goes by without the Department of Justice entering suits or complaints against half a dozen or more market conspirators.

The original Anti-Trust enactment, the Sherman Act of 1890, is little more than a restatement of the Anglo American Common Law. Monopoly, except in special cases as for certain industries classified as public utilities is outlawed as a moral as well as economic matter. Conspiracy, for any reason, is outlawed.

The conspiracy issue is a fairly obvious one. For individuals to combine their efforts, in a clandestine manner, to gain certain ends which might be proper for individuals to attain, is anathema as an economic and ethical matter. Raising prices by a single seller is quite different from a dozen sellers agreeing to raise prices. Conspiracy restricts the freedom of other individuals, buyers or sellers, to do their business effectively. Therefore it is illegal. If individuals form a corporation, and receive a charter or license from the State authority, the action not only is known, the requirements of corporate behavior are constrained, restrained and required by law and by administrative rule. Competitors providing substitutes may be hurt if the corporation is successful, but the hurt is done openly and by legitimated means.

For a joint action to be undertaken on the sly, or by conspiracy, i.e. without at least implicit governmental sanction, with the limits of the conspirational action unrestrained, then the hurt to competitors and to competition is illegal. If the actors, operating several independent firms, conspire to fix prices and in general act against public policy, the acts and the operation are illegal. Whether or not the conspiratorial action increases or decreases the G.N.P. or the social welfare is irrelevant. The social and economic risk of conspiracy is too great for society to bear. The risk of market danger is sufficiently great to outlaw conspiracy. The operative word is "outlaw". Conspiracy is by definition, or *"per se,"* as American courts have it, illegal because of its deficiencies for the whole society and potential competitors. Public policy is invaded. Government is denigrated.

A single seller of a good gives that seller a greater power to fix price or output than were there a number of competitors. Thus consumers as well as potential competitors are disbenefitted. And this is generally politically and socially viewed as evil. *In recent years the political process of the economically powerful is viewed as a potential threat to the political and social system.* Hence there is an additional moral basis for anti monopoly legislation.

The idea of monopoly in law is not necessarily a single producer or seller, rather it pertains to a market in which there are a few sellers, who thus can segregate and/or control the market shares. The law is generally concerned with market control and regulation by authorities other than those regulated and approved by the State. Lacking hard and fast rules which define what may or may not be, the courts are guided by the "Rule of Reason". The American courts judge the appropriateness of market behavior by what the courts consider reasonable or unreasonable behavior, limited by *per se* and statutory considerations.

The possibility that economies of scale might lead to monopoly is sometimes allowed in that public utilities are expressly allowed to be monopolies, or practical monopolies, but only with price, output and often quality regulation by government. In the United States there is a blurring of the public utility boundaries. Transport, communications, mail services, some aspects of education, are in the process of evolving from monopolistic or partial monopolistic activities, either public or private, to less regulated and hopefully less monopolized undertakings. Both the moral legitimation and the technical-economic aspects are undergoing perception changes in the public eye. Even a state monopoly stands the chance of losing some of the advantages in a competitive system. There is a tradeoff. The U.S. Postal Service is besieged by private delivery firms. American Telephone and Telgraph willingly gave up its monopoloid position because of the competition of substitute technologies and a desire to enter other industries.

There is thus a statutory, moral and economic basis for Anti Trust extending from monopoly to merger and acquisitions, from price fixing and other evidences of conspiracy directed to market control via market share. Courts in America sometimes justify the law by arguing that the ideal is not to protect competitors. This is a high sounding declaration but, in truth competitors – buyers and sellers – are protected to the degree that competition is protected.

As one would expect, not every interest group in society is likely to hold the same views on market restraints imposed by law. Anti trust and other market regulations are indeed market restraints because they limit free action in the marketplace. Such laws and regulations are constraints insofar as they require certain actions in the marketplace.[5]

4 Self Interest is a Reason

Large scale producers, be they final goods producers such as automobile manufacturers, or makers of producer goods as steel, have a different view of government regulatory policy than, say, the suppliers to such firms or small firms generally. All firms in the trucking and building industries do not view regulations which protect their activities e.g. special licenses and area limitations for trucking, and building codes for the building industry, as unduly restrictive. Indeed such firms, and the labor unions in them, often tend to be supportive of restrictive legislation. A preferred market position akin to monopoly does not require a large market share if law and regulations are sufficiently protective. The attitude of individuals toward restricitive legislation, we suggest, rests on the interest of the person and on his or her situation in the market. Interests are related to perceived actual or anticipated benefits. Perceptions may be correct or incorrect, but the benefit of the person is a major self concern.

Self interest, however, or selfishness in a narrow sense, are not the only values which motivate behavior. All of us, in varying degrees, hold to values which are not reflections of maximum self interest. The views we hold on acts in all their manifestations vary from the very petty to the very general. For a public administrator to apply a ruling on, say, a minor real estate use variance, may be a usual, really unimportant action. But a variance on use from residential to commercial may be a major issue for the community and in the moral thoughts of the administrator. Morality, in all its varied manifestations may vary from matters of small moment e.g. rote politeness, to the consideration of ideals of enormous dimensions, e.g. water pollution. All the varied considerations need not and presumably are not only related to our self interests. A plant located in A or B might be equally productive. But A is a depressed community and B a prosperous one. In terms of the manager's self interest location at A or B is indifferent. But the choice, in terms of social welfare or perceived need, may imply an ethical consideration.

Our passions, aesthetics and ethics are embraced without total regard for income or power. To be sure we often trade off the realization of our passionately held values and ideals for our material interests. But we also trade off one interest for another. Salary is forgone for leisure or a less demanding career, security is traded off for interesting challenges. So our passionate interest say in music is forgone sometimes because the price of a concert ticket is too high, or the weather is inclement. Our ideals of human dignity are set aside as we take advantage of foreign goods made by underpaid, exploited labor. But, on the other hand a passion for art or a deep concern for civil liberties or education may entail contributions and costs which are not offset by any personal benefit except the feeling that one has aided some worthwhile cause. In World War I Americans did not listen to Wagner's music because it wasn't played. In World War II movies, plays and novels sympathetic to the Soviet struggle were hits, far beyond any artistic worth. Art, politics and self interest are curiously complex.

Our material interests, generally speaking, can be expressed in some (money) quantitative terms as income flows or capital funds. We use logic and language to manipulate and communicate ideas about all our interests. This manipulation and communication *via* logic is less applicable to the consideration of values which comprehend aesthetics and morals. Then persuasion becomes more important. Who is to say that Monet is a better artist than Munch, or that child labor is a greater social misfortune than the unemployment of young people? To be sure as aesthetic values are codified by writings and conventions, artists are classified and put into hierarchical gradings.

The morality of business and market behavior, however, remain highly personal manifestations aside from the conventions and arbitrary ordering of legalistic values. Business executives are not supposed to, and in past do not, discuss their price policy with competitors, and decide which alternative is better or worse. To do so not only would be in possible violation of law, it would be in violation of the individualistic spirit which is a powerful force in the U.S. As we have suggested, moral actions are personally considered by the actor in question as tensions between personally held values and the actor's interpretation or evaluation of what he or she considers the behavior (values) which the time and place expect of him or her.

5 Rote Behavior and Tension

By our argument ethical actions tend to be more immediate than general, bound by time circumstance.[6] Rules (or laws), as we use the concept, imply some categorical imperative of obedience. They are, one might say surrogates of natural law. One does not usually abstain from stealing because of considerations by which one weighs the chances of being caught against not being caught, and concludes that the risks attendant upon stealing are simply too great. Such rationality is unusual, and would apply only to the rational man of economic theory who had moved over to a world of robbery.

Generally speaking, I suggest, we refrain from stealing because we have been taught to believe stealing is morally wrong or better still is "just not done". The tension within us between wanting to steal and the idea that we are not expected to steal is in most circumstances below the threshold of current experience or moral wrestling. Yet if placed in a strange or novel situation where our notions of what is expected are not clear, and the opportunity for appropriating some object fairly good, then stealing occurs. In World War II appropriating goods in enemy and also friendly territory was widespread among American soldiers from high officers to the rank and file. Indeed the accepted term was "liberating" the goods in question. The inner tension simply was not there. Once when I was working in the U.S. Embassy in Great Britain a special emergency meeting of an international committee on which I sat was called on a holiday, a Saturday or Sunday. The meeting was in the British Foreign Office, or some such place of decorous distinction. I noticed virtually every member ot the Committee "liberated" a pen or some other small item from the table, no doubt as a souvenir. The propriety of the action was simply not an issue.

Thou shalt not kill, or thou shalt not steal, or love your neighbor as yourself, or don't (or do) blow the whistle, or don't (or do) take advantage of a trading partner's weakness, or do (or don't) charge what the traffic will bear, etc. really are not by themselves very useful ethical guides. The socialization and internalization of these ideas control personal behavior. Morality is usually learned not imposed. It is not measured by the yardstick of efficiency.

6 The Uniqueness of the Ethical Act

In the United States, during the past decade or so there has developed great interest in business ethics. I relate it to the Watergate and post Watergate exposures of government and business chicanery. Many new courses have been offered in business and professional schools dealing with what essentially is the ethics of the marketplace. Such courses have often consisted, first of a quick overview of ethics as developed by philosophers, stretching from deontology to situational ethics. The course then is directed toward "cases". Real or hypothetical situations are presented to the students for discussion. Questions of employment of woman and racial minorities are presented, as are such questions of industrial pricing, whistle blowing, and quality control. In short social questions on which a firm's management may take, or has taken, a position are presented and analyzed.

Two comments are in order from one who has taught such courses.

1 There is the distinct possiblity that the student and teacher may fall into the trap of deciding that there is a single definable, ethical solution not only to the problem at hand, but to similar problems which may arise. After all a case is meaningful only as it prepares one to solve similar cases. The scientist doesn't cut open a dog to learn what is in the dog. He cuts

open the dog to learn what is in dogs he does not cut open. The epistemology of ethics may be different.

As we have argued, ethical problems tend to be unique, particular, to the actor whether he is the observer, manager or an involved or uninvolved employee. Generalization is meaningful only to the degree that observer and actor share in the conception of what conventional behavior is, and what the moral tensions *within* the actor or observer are. In the classroom rarely does a student sense a novel set of tensions. More likely than not student and teacher, possibly led by the teacher, come up with a congruence of moral tension which probably is quite noncongruent with the tensions felt by real actors, if the case were a real one. The moral judgment of the class may be inapropos to the relevant moral judgment. At best it is a social criticism based on the values of student and teacher, with relevant facts and attitudes probably missing and without an analytic understanding. I suggest that the analytic understanding is of greater heuristic value than an *ad hoc* moral judgment. Real moral issues do not always or even often carry over from one situation to another. Soldiers, politicians, physicians, business and trade union leaders and others who have been engaged in heroic actions often feel that crities on the sidelines simply do not understand the nature of the heroic act.

2 The second weakness of the case method of understanding ethical behavior is more subtle. Many of the cases, in my experience, often the more interesting cases, are law suits. A firm did thus which the courts (usually the U.S. Supreme Court) found proper (or improper), and allowed (or disallowed) the action. The class then analyzes the court ruling in the light of the economic theory involved, the ethical preconceptions of class and teacher and the political or ideological currents. The motives generating the business action are usually considered clear, even self evident. For example, it is generally assumed the Ford Motor Company did not strengthen the Pinto's rear end because it would cost too much. In point of fact, in the hindsight at least, the loss due to the bad publicity was probably many times the cost of protecting the gasoline tanks which were poorly engineered. That the fault may have lain in the *managerial structure* of Ford, and in weakness of its *interdepartment communications system,* or in some other aspect than direct cost is rarely suggested. (At least I have never seen it suggested.) Again the moral judgment of the class is probably not based on a correct technical and moral set of assumptions underlying the behavior of the Ford Motor Company. Questions of motives need to be properly specified.

To further obfuscate the interesting and, to my mind, relevant issues in an ethical discussion, the case method tends to confuse legal behavior with ethical behavior. To the extent that the meaning and application of the law is known, the obvious course of action of the firm is to obey the law. The decision and responsibility is that of management, personalized for ease of exposition into "the manager." He, this hypothetical manager, can delegate authority but not responsibility. If the meaning and application of the law is not certain, then the lawyers, the mouthpieceas and paid best friends of the manager, suggest the probability of success of a given course of action, that is to say success in law court not in the marketplace. Market success is in the purview of the manager not the lawyer.[7] The ethical issues facing the managers are, by going to court, reduced to legal issues. The law is or is not broken, or the law is immoral. Yet the real issue is the action of the manager.

No ethical values are being tested. The rough guide to the manager is efficiency–maximization of profits within the socially accepted limits of behavior. If the courts approve the action, the manager and his lawyer are justified, if not, then they are wrong. In circumstances in which risks are taken in the firm's name, or novel undertakings experimented with, the manager is the responsible person. If the owners object they can remove the manager. If the majority of ownership approves, the manager may continue. He *is* responsible management until removed by the owners or by law.

For our purposes then the ethics of the firm are the ethics of the manager (short for management). His ethical actions, as we define them, are beyond and above the required and assumed required limits of law or managerial rules of business and of market behavior. The manager's ethical decisions become the policy and practice of the firm in so far as his authority is as effective as is his unavoidable responsibility. But, in the complexity and often confusion of administration, authority and responsibility are not congruent. In a sense ethical correction of the market may be supportive of ideas of fairness and justice, if these are somehow lacking. In 1982 the U.S. Department of Justice changed its guide lines of merger structure. Business behavior and conventional market morality changed. Private market morality presumably also changed. Mergers became more daring.

7 Responsibility is Persistent

Authority in an organization may be delegated by plan as well as by circumstance. The manager of even a small firm of 50 or 100 employees, even of less than 50, does not personally supervise every phase of operations, or make every decision. Judgment is always and inevitably exercised by subordinates. A major problem of administration is how to channel and constrain judgments so that they conform to the firm's policy as well as to public law and convention.

Administrative lack of coordination can lead the officials of the firm to behavior not in accord with firm policy or with legal and conventional requirements. It is also possible that as a matter of policy management may have decided to pursue a line of behavior which does not comport with law or convention. The deviation from law, convention or from policy may occur because of judgments (or ignorance) at many levels of corporate administration. Such deviations may involve behavior which the manager, observer, or affected person considers illegal or unethical.

Responsibility in many cases must be borne by the manager, but not in all cases. The supervisor who, in spite of policy directions, breaks the law with respect, let us say, to hours of work of empolyees, or who falsified records to make his operation appear more successful than it is, should as a matter of morality bear the blame. The managers at the upper reaches are, however, responsible for righting any wrong and instituting an effective managerial structure. As a general rule obedience to law is an obligation of the manager and hence of the firm. This obligation assumes (or requires) an organization which permits the free flow of information within the system, and also is conducive to managerial awareness. The left hand must know what the right hand is up to. Ethical judgment may lead top management as well as subordinates to depart from rules. As an outside case, a firm in Hitler's Germany would have acted ethically, from the viewpoint of most foreign observers and many Germans, if the management, at any level, disobeyed and got around Nazi rules, policies and laws concerned with racial, religious, political, and various other discriminatory strictures. Such ethical behavior, we say, is an outside case because the societies of the Western World that we are concerned with, rarely rely on such cruel and blatant attempts as did the Nazis. Western governments and business generally speaking may really want to be even handed and to eliminate discrimination.

The world of our concern is subtle, even sophisticated in how it exercises its biases. The great American social revaluation of the '60s and '70s marked the end of the era of obvious and often publicly accepted social discrimination. It also was a period in which a society was made self conscious of its internal shortcomings by the Watergate and post Watergate exposes of the 1970s. The "rights" of minorities, which is to say the acceptance into the economic system, at levels consonant with their skill and ability, of women, Blacks, Hispanics and other minority groups became the concern of Congress, the Administration, the Courts and a wide public. The problems of such discrimination have not been solved, nor are effective solutions known; but the new ethical or social ethical thrust is to recognize the issues and seek equitable solutions. The task is formidable.

The Reagan departure from the administrative ideology of past administrations' equal rights policy has not captured the imagination of a large part, of the people of the U.S. There seems to be a consciousness, however, to a greater degree than in the past 50 years, of the desirability of competition, safety, health, and various market accomodations with respect to price and quality. The new self consciousness applies to a host of other real and possible deviations from the policy of stressing market efficiency. Even the Reagan Administration which originally won public support by the plea to "get government off our backs" was forced by the same public's pressure to maintain many of the market interventionistic and "entitlement" policies of former Administrations. Attempts to tinker with Social Security and pollution control brought that message home to the Reagan Administration and to Republicans generally.

Business and government are, in a sense, constantly being exposed to ethical scrutiny. Many firms and public administrations have set up special agencies to police their inner workings. The press has become sensitive to stories of private and public misadventure. And then there is the phenomenon of "whistle blowing". Whistle blowing is the term used to define an employee's publicizing through the press, congressional committees, and other public fora, lapses of policy or behavior within an enterprise, private or public.

Whistle blowing has occurred in U.S. Government departments, in large corporations, in banks, indeed in many large institutions. The Department of Defense has been accused before congressional committees of overpaying contractors for material, of renegotiating contracts to compensate contractors who have had unjustified cost overruns and who in general were not very efficient nor honest. Stupidly the Department, in some instances, tried to punish the ethically or otherwise inspired whistle blowers. Whistle blowing employees were dismissed, demoted and otherwise punished even though, prior to the public exposure, responsible Departmental officials had been apprised of the lapses. The result was congressional investigation, law suits to protect whistle blowers, and various noises of reform. It is, however, not clear that the problems have been solved or that policy and law are markedly better enforced.[8] The 1985 exposés of extremely improper and questionable behavior in the Department of Defense, led the D.O.D. to take action against contractors and department officials who were involved in the mess. Eight hundred dollar toilet seats are too uncomfortable for taxpayers.

The ethical implications of whistle blowing have caught the fancy of academic and professionally involved writers. By and large academics tend to support the ethics of whistle blowing, but only *after* the appropriate internal to the firm procedures have been followed. Some business experts, Peter Drucker among them, however agree that after the internal warnings have been made, the whistle blower should remain quiet. The harm to the organization flow of authority, it seems to be alleged, is generally speaking, greater than the immediate benefits of correcting a particular inequity. As we pointed out, the focus of analysis often is in the legality of whistle blowing and on the issue of whether there is a social and private bias for or against such public disclosure.

The evaluation of a whistle blowing case, as of any case of ethical business practice, we feel, should be in terms of; "What are the likely implications of the particular action?" Whistle blowing cases tend to make the issue the *whistle blower*. But he or she is *not* the essential ethical issue. That is to be found in the subject and substance of what is being exposed.

To blow the whistle on an issue of, let us say, the improper firing of one employee out of a work force of 1,000 is a lesser issue than the firm's systematic refusal to hire qualified women or Blacks. The social and personal implication of the former action is less than of the latter. To be sure *neither* is justified. To be sure steps should be taken internally to correct the wrong. But every issue cannot be, and should not be, exposed to public gaze lest the firm lose the public's confidence, spend its time and money defending itself, and have its inner discipline erode. Just where the point which separates public disclosure from the continuance of private wrong cannot be made in the abstract or on a general basis. Each case of whistle blowing has to be justified or not justified on the basis of the issues and implications of the issues of that *particular* case.[9]

As an analogy, the U.S. Government has followed a policy of denying all federal funds to a university which does not conform to any single anti discrimination rule. Thus if the university's academic department of accounting is found guilty by the Government administering agency of a discriminatory bias, the university may then be denied funds for research in physics or funds for helping impoverished students.

Tying together a discrimination case in accounting with funds for physics research seems to create a flow of implications which are not the relevant ones to consider, if anti discrimination is the object of the exercise. The punitive exercise does not correct the wrong, but it has punished many people who were neither guilty nor were they accessories.

Our own suggestion is that the appropriate role of government should be determined by considerations which are (a) programmatic, and (b) in accord with the value systems as expressed by legislatures, courts, and administrators, by the custom of the institutions in question, and by the attitudes of faculty, students, trustees, et. al. Judgment in these cases ultimately rests with government. There is no absolute rule, there is no clear cut right and wrong. Not only is *autres temps, autres moeurs* at work, but what is ultimately wanted has to be considered. The posited ends often determine the means. The employment of German rocket experts and scientists after World War II by the U.S. government and by the Soviet government illustrate this pragmatic attitude toward ethics. Self interest tends to be present in ethical decisions, but ideas of justice, fairness and generosity are also strong. In brief our conception of ethics in the market is related to the idea of legal realism. What happens, outside of specific regulations is that an actor tries to do what he or she somehow believes should be done in accordance with the spirit and intent of the law and accepted ideas of justice and fairness.

The ethical considerations of government administrators, and of others involved in the decision making, it seems to me, can be structured in a sequential fashion similar to the following:

1 the awareness of an expected "ethical" procedure in a particular situation in which choices are open to the actors,
2 the belief that, from the viewpoint of an actor's self interest and his passions i.e. values independent of self interest, alternative actions are possible,
3 the choosing of one line of action from several, and so reduce the tension brought about by the value or ethical tension in the individual.

The first comment need not be, and often is not, perceived by the individual as a finely defined perception. Alternative values on the social scene themselves have to be weighed. For example a firm is faced with the problem of retrenching. The manager recognizes, from a technical viewpoint, that costs cannot be allowed to exceed income for the ensuing period. But there are alternative ways of cutting costs. Workers may be laid off, wages or other costs may be cut, unprofitable lines may be cut. With layoffs of labor and increases in idle capacity, loans can be sought, merger or sale of the company may be undertaken, an advertising program may be instituted and so on. The considerations contemplate technical and procedural alternative impacts on labor, shareholders, community, managers, buyers, sellers, etc. The technical and procedural considerations are not included in any value or ethical consideration, but provide the basis for estimating the alternative implications to the several groups which would be affected.

The second point is the analytic process which further applies the analysis of (1) to particular groups and persons. "If we do this then that will happen." Choices as to the most desired outcomes are exposed, and choices are made. In (2) the manager is choosing who will be hurt and who benefitted. What he views as the behavior "expected" of him may be followed, amended or discarded in the light of his own interests and passions (values).

The third consideration, knowledge and analysis, plus the reliance on experience, insight and hunch are what we may call, for want of a better term, the reflective basis of action. But it can have relevance only insofar as the reflection is based on some value system or structure which the manager-actor believes he understands, or which he posits. His behavior is purposive not rote. The action is purposive and concerned with direct and indirect implications.

Now there are degrees of departure from what we have considered expected behavior, even if such behavior appears as a set of alternatives. The choice of one line of behavior from several, is a willed, free choice act. The comparison between that combined technical-value guide or yardstick and the details and configuration of the action the manager chooses to take in the particular situation is another act of free will, including, of course, the firm's departure from the perception of what the guide or yardstick suggests. The guide might be the law, or it might be a convention or conception less rigorously defined and less sharply outlined than a statute or legal precedent. At any rate the manager makes a choice. If he has no choice, or believes he has no choice, there are no ethical overtones to the exercise.

The manager may, as a usual rule, avoid any ethical departures from perceived norms of behavior. One who closely follows the rules avoids ethical decisions. "Working to rules" is a way government workers sometimes strike! Generally the behavior of managers, supervisors and other employees is in accordance with rule and precedent. Something happens and the actor reacts almost out of second nature. Choices are ethically neutral, for example, if the manager is borrowing funds. He looks at the terms of loan, interest rates, and other technical considerations offered by several sources. He chooses the best from the viewpoint of self interest of the firm.

But all choices are not neutral with respect to implications. That is where the technical choices are conditioned by the implications of the possible alternatives. Whom does the manager want to help or hinder, what purposes has he, other than merely the technical ones? Such choices go even further. What if the manger is insecure about what he believes the firm is doing? He may feel that a given line of activity, although profitable, is socially suspect. For example the product may be dysfunctional.

I know a business man who was offered, and was about to accept the post of president of a large cigarette manufacturing company. When he told his wife and grown children of the offer the children objected to the point of threatening to have nothing to do with the father if he took the job! After a week of depression and soul searching he refused the offer. In effect he was a dropout from the cigarette trade not because of self interest in the conventional economic sense, but because of the passions and values of his family. He went with a wine importing firm!

If a person is so disaffected by the tensions between perceived values and internally held values, he may drop out of the business system entirely. How many successful businessmen do just that and take up, late in life, careers in academia only to find that the ethical tensions in academia are no less than in business? The stakes are less, but the lower and fewer stakes and economic rewards possibly may make the competition for the limited prizes even sharper than in the more conventional economic market. The ultimate business ethical dropout, one incorrectly might suppose, would be the conversion from business management to some sort of nonbusiness management. Enterprises of art, religion or revolution may not be business but they have their rationalities and their own quantities to be optimized.

In the normal range of ethical affairs we suggest that value choices are constrained by fairly well defined limits of technical knowledge and capacity, and by fairly well defined groups or persons to be benefitted– e.g. workers, shareholders, buyers, and sellers. What is interesting is that under different circumstances the ethical significance of the hierarchy of persons to be benefitted shifts. Employment considerations are more important in a recession than in prosperity; inflation tends to emphasize issues of prices and buyers, and so on. This leads me to suggest that (self) interest, seen as managerial and thus firm interest, is almost always intertwined with ethical interests. Ethics becomes one of the elements in decision making. Therefore the analytic and reflective procedures determining policy and practice, to be most useful, should, insofar as possible, include an overt value component. Unless this is done, the value component will be introduced subconsciously, or at least without being consciously formulated and its implications weighed.

Ethics is nothing if it is not freely chosen and consciously legitimated. Chance or necessity are not elements in moral choice. Ethics is not to be legitimated (hence communicated) as a technical requirement and necessity. It is *not* a costless characteristic of behavior. If ethical values are of great value, how can one expect them to be costless? Things of value are rare, and often their value is in some proportion to their rarity.

8 Ethical Acts as Deviant

Ethical actions then are deviations from rule and law, consciously undertaken, and with a cost to the enterprise. Ethical considerations are not absolute but subject to tradeoffs, and are reasonably chosen. Reasonable choice implies that the ends are worth the effort. The worth of ethical goals, however, is not subject to the same measures as the worth of economic goals, which may be quantitatively measured. This, as we have argued, makes it difficult to talk about, explain, and justify ethical ends and their costs.

But we must and do in fact argue about, defend, attack and embrace goals which cannot be compared to other goals except on the basis of persuasion rather than logic and rationality. Removing ethics from the absolute does not render the idea entirely personal, hence relative, or as some theologians would have it, situational. To the extent that there is a common value heritage, a common social and educational structure there is a commonality of ethical views. Indeed a society functions well to the extent that the spectrum of ethical values is limited and more or less commonly held. Ethical considerations, especially new ones may be disruptive. But disruption is part of the social dynamic.

When the social world is unruly and disordered, the analytic reflective processes become more numerous among observers. Varied theories "explain" the world, and its directions and equilibrium become debatable. Then the value system tends to change. Both the analytic systems and the perceptions of what is needed to make life tolerable doubtless affect the ethical value systems. To the degree that the world is morally homogeneous and stable, then the alternativies of ethical behavior become fewer and more similar to each other. The world also may become dull.

Ours is a world of change. Our arbitrary worlds of business, of the western culture, and of traditional values are always in flux, but more so in recent years than, say, in the last century. This assertion of current instability may be a conceit because every time and place considers itself as undergoing extraordinary travail. But our society does seem to face pressures and threats which appear both novel and powerful. Africa Asia, the Soviet Union, South America as well as the highly developed lands, all feel great external and internal pressures of an ethical and political nature. The ethical values of a society are likely to react to the threats and accomplishments of the times.

This is not strange for *"Nihil manet sed mutandum,"* nothing is constant but change, is as true now as ever it was.

Footnotes

[1] T. Beauchamp and N. Bowie – *Ethical Theory and Business*, Prentice Hall, 1979, p. 130 ff.
[2] Ibid, p. 125 ff.
[3] R. DeGeorge – "Utility and Utilitarianism," Ch. 3 in *Business Ethics*, McMillan, 1982.
[4] S. C. Sufrin – "How Moral Can A Business Be?" *Christian Century*, 1983.
[5] I. Millstein and S. Katsch – *Limits of Corporate Power*, see Ch. II "Economic Constraints," McMillan, 1981.
[6] G. Brand – *The Essential Wittgenstein*, Sec. VIII, p. 165 ff, Basic Books, 1979.
[7] G. Lodge – "The Ethical Implications of Ideology," Ch. 4 in *Business Ethics*, W. Hoffman & J. Moore, Ed., McGraw Hill, 1984.
[8] G. Lodge – Ibid. 157 ff.
[9] J. Thomson – "Preferential Hiring," *Philosophy & Public Affairs, II #4, 1973*.

Chapter IV
The Market Ethic and Relevance

1 Legitimation

The economic ideal of conservatives tends to be a concern with the size of the national dividend. The bigger the GNP the more successful the market society. Liberals, on the other hand, tend to be concerned with size *and* distribution of GNP. Income maximization is less important than a tolerable GNP distributed in some morally acceptable fashion.

Generally speaking we justify any social undertaking by at least two criteria: (1) pragmatic considerations and (2) moral content.

1 The *first* criterion of justification is "Will what we are trying to do work?" Some medicines work better than others, some don't work at all, while still others make our situation worse. But the ability of a course of action to achieve the ends sought is often not enough. We are also concerned with what the medical profession calls "side effects", with what some economists call "neighborhood effects," and others call "externalities" or "market failures". In short even if an action does what it was planned to do, it also may have other effects, good or bad, outside the area of desired action. Such side, neighborhood or external reactions must, in many aspects of social action, be included in any evaluation or legitimation of the action. An act, however, which is successful in doing what the actor wants done, and whose externalities are known beforehand by analysis, is nevertheless not automatically legitimated.

2 This leads to the *second* criterion of legitimation, namely the ethical or moral content. To blow up a munitions dump and thereby destroy all equipment stored in a 500 foot radius may be the goal of a military airplane pilot. He may achieve a hit with 100% efficiency. But a full social legitimation is still lacking. The action may be legitimate and moral in the ideology of the military undertaking and institution. But to a pacifist, or

even the enemy of the attacking pilot, an ethical legitimation is not so easily forthcoming.

The business world is not the world of the military. Business is concerned with achieving some well defined goals, as well as others which are not so well defined. Business also generates externalities which may be important to other elements in the society, externalities which may be beneficial or harmful. Business operates generally speaking on a costs versus returns basis by which money costs and money returns are compared. But to those involved as managers, employees, competitors, government administrators, investors, and so on, other considerations than money costs and returns also play roles of differing significance at different times.

The means and the externalities of the action to achieve the goal often have ethical dimensions. It is our purpose to discuss some of the characteristics of these ethical dimensions. What we shall *not* attempt is to define a set of specific values which we consider as absolutely applicable, or a set of practices which we consider uniquely able to achieve high ethical results. Rather we shall concern ourselves with discussing the structure of an ethical system in the market, and the alternative moral aspects of the structure. The alternatives are neither limitless nor unique to any person. Ethical behavior and ethical outcomes are social in nature, and so are shared. They are also limited to time and place.

At the onset a caveat is necessary. Since, in our view, ethical behavior and ethical outcomes are not absolute, criticism of behavior and outcomes, from the moral standpoint, are inevitable. We all have the capacity to criticize the moral implications of any act. When the moral critique is directed at an action taken within time and action frames which are common both to the critic and the actions and ideology, the relevance of the criticism is apparent. But when the criticism is directed against an historical action, or an action in a place and among people markedly different from the critic's time, place, and society, the argument is sometimes made that such criticism is irrelevant.

Surely criticism of any sort, of a here and now action, or of an action undertaken in some far off place and far off time – may be irrelevant. By irrelevant I mean not applicable, unrevealing and missing the point. To point out as a criticism of, say, an Administration's fiscal policy, or of the opposition's tax suggestions, it seems to me, may be both valid and relevant. But criticisms of the administration's stance on the budgetary deficit by some pundits may be less than relevant because of the technical ignorance and powerful political difficulties of solving the only vaguely perceived and very complex problem. The criticism may be valid-steps to reduce the deficit are essential, but irrelevant-for no one really is sure how to do it; or better there are so many alternatives, and such a great spread of possible social costs that a consensus is lacking. Reducing the deficits is sure to hurt some blameless people.

Similarly one may inveigh against some political and social policies of some African states, or of India, or of the Soviet Union. Often the criticisms are valid-e.g. governments should not condone violence against people, or graft, or discrimination, but the criticisms may also be irrelevant because of the incapacity of government to alleviate much less solve the problem, and because the ideologies in question may not comport with the ideology of the critics. Whether or not South African whites find apartheid ethical, the foreign observer may find it offensive. Its legality is of no ethical concern.

Academic and other learned folk who argue of the rights and wrongs of what happened in ancient Greece or in the Middle Ages are scarcely moralistic, in any applicable sense. Nor are they necessarily humanists. They are historians of events which had a moral element. Only if the analysis points to some generalized idea about moral structure can the historical analysis be considered as a moral analysis or as humanistic.

Current events clearly have moral overtones. The messes in Beirut, nuclear armament, even tax and budget matters have elements of truth, goodness and beauty in them or as implications. The moral elements become, in most notions, the parameters of the discussion and program. From one viewpoint a major task of ethics as a discipline is to expose the structure of ethics.

Acceptance, in general, of the pragmatic view, requires I believe, the acceptance, in any particular instance, that the ability to solve or at least alleviate the perceived problem at hand must be within the power of the actor or other actors. Only then can an ethical evaluation be made of the solution.

Our orientation is toward the ethics of markets and market economics. Thus matters of a personal or familial nature are not overtly considered, although I believe that the critical limitations suggested above are applicable. Wayward children are admittedly a pain to parents and society. But who knows what to do to correct waywardness? But in market settings, we are really discussing policy – macro policy – usually with respect to government or some other authority e.g. a trade association or a very large firm which dominates a market. Micro policy is only the policy of a firm operating in a market.

2 Management

In the following observations and discussions of behavior we shall assume that the firm at the micro level, or authority at the macro level, are personalized by the term manager (or management) and government or administration. We realize, of course, that a single individual rarely makes decisions which control an entire institution. Decisions are made jointly by individuals in charge, some minor ones are made by individuals and supported or not revoked by superiors in the organization, some are made by subordinates with little or no review.

However a decision to act when alternative actions are available to secure the same goal, or decisions to choose an immediate goal, with or without alternative means being available, are different from a rote action. Such action might *seem* as if it involves choice on the part of the actor. For our purposes such rote or required actions, whether of means or ends, are not considered free choice actions, and thus are devoid of any moral implication. However the manager may be guilty of unethical behavior if he fails to notice the moral implications and the alternatives available to him, and he relies on rote behavior only because it "is always done that way". One availability is to stop what is being done, and do nothing. Even doing nothing may have grave implications of a moral sort. The manager who always follows the ways of the past is neither a good manager nor an especially ethical person.

Currently the industrial and the non industrial worlds are concerned with pollution of the air, the land and water. Negative externalities-disbenefits-may flow from unethical behavior by some industries and firms, as well as from ill conceived technical aspects of policy implementation. Let us take the case of Love Canal in the Buffalo area of New York State. A chemical company dumped steel drums of noxious chemicals into an unfinished, unused canal which it owned and filled in the ditch with dirt. Years later, after the land had been given to the city and subsequently sold to real estate developers who built and sold homes on the site, householders began to fall ill. Their cellars leaked poisons and other unpleasant events occurred. The problems were traced to the chemical dump. The area was closed to use. The question of legal liability is for courts to decide. The ethical question, however, is also intriguing.

Is the management of the chemical company responsible? Did it act without a proper concern? And was the state of the arts sufficiently advanced at the time of the original dumping to provide a warning or clue to the future? Were the City Fathers guilty of an unethical act in selling the contaminated land which the company gave to the city? Should the buyers of the land have investigated the nature of the landfill? Hindsight may pose questions to which foresight is blind because one does not expect surprises in routine matters. Surprises are only fun when they are beneficial. Neither negative nor positive surprises are expected. That is obvious. But how investigative should one be in a fairly routine operation? If it can be shown that knowledge or even a hint of knowledge about the potential dangers of the Love Canal site was suppressed by any donor or seller, then a case of immoral (and probably illegal) action can be made.

What we are again suggesting is that technology (or technique) and ethics are combined in many business undertakings, with ethics not being a pressing issue in the normal run of events. (We obviously are neglecting the position of those who would argue that capitalism, or business, or markets or any economic institutions extant in the West, are *per se* and by definition immoral. This point of view is, in our view, irrelevant whether valid or not.)

Relevant criticism of behavior however can be made at the macro and micro levels, from the points of view of buyers, sellers, manufacturers, labor, government administration, even by observers, including those trained and untrained in the arts of business, economics, and administration. The criticisms may be moral, aesthetic or technical in their orientation.

The Greek idea of dividing the ideal behavior of the world and its reactions to truth, goodness and beauty is still a good way to divide the ongoingness of the world for purposes of study and evaluation. Truth, goodness and beauty comprehend the moral, aesthetic and technical aspects of the world we live in, including the market. Aesthetics has not generally been applied to market phenomenon. Yet ideas and ideals of beauty do apply. In the Bauhaus period of art and architecture the essence of the use of a product and the production process itself were symbolically represented in structure, strength and mass of the final product. This was the basis of the architecture, furniture, and representational art which flourished in the Bauhaus era of post World War I to World War II.Both before and after the Bauhaus movement the production and products themselves were and are often endowed with niceties and elegance which are aesthetic. Use alone, or efficiency alone, are not persistent marks of human artifacts, relationships or endeavors.

3 The Perception of Ethical Behavior

But to return to the main line of argument. If ethics is an integral part of human activity and if ethics is ultimately based on a freely willed act by an individual, are ethical precepts like other social phenomena? Our affirmative answer is based on a theory or assumption of perception. Basically the theory is directed to answer two questions:

1 How does one acquire the belief that doing one thing is *morally* better than doing another?
2 If ethical views are personal how is it that there is such general agreement on what is moral, and what is not, in given situations?

Our view is that the individuals' values and perceptions are gathered from the experiences, direct and vicarious, of his world impinging on his consciousness, which is unique to him. The reality of the world is taken for granted. That the external world exists is an heroic assumption, which includes the minor assumption that it is an ordered and is a cause and effect world. Whether it is or not we can never know. If it has an existence, *independent* of the individual, we can never know. But we accept whatever it is that we perceive, and let its existence go at that. What does concern us is its past, its future, its operation. This view may be essentially solipsistic, with other people and their views being part of the perceived world. But these other people seem to have perceptions not too dissimilar to our own, and they seem to react to the signals we send them and vice versa. That is to say communication seems to take place. The communication is most comprehensible when it is constrained by logic, number and other mechanical or highly ordered signals. Logic and grammar, the necessary relations and the order of such relations, seem to be more comprehended and comprehensible than rhetoric. What we call truth, that is some verifiable and nonrefuted but refutable proposition, relies probably more on logic and grammar than on rhetoric. But rhetoric, with its component of logic and grammar is more a feature of the persuasiveness of aesthetics and ethics than of truth.

The world, then, is assumed as a generally ordered generator of experience, the individual as a receptor of the world's signals. In the world are other individuals (by assumption) who too receive signals, and can, in turn, communicate with each other and with the individual we started with (the us or I, if you will).

The individual is like a radar antenna moving in a 360 arc, and analyzing the signals by his mind, which is a radar set of differing quality and efficiency for each of us. In the antenna's twirling it picks up signals from (presumably) other antennae, and so communication occurs.

Let us drop the analogy and return to human individuals. We live in a world and what is more we can communicate, that is (consciously and unconsciously) affect and be affected by other people and by events. In brief we have smuggled a kind of free will into this big complex of assumptions for we act *as if* we can choose how and what to communicate and affect. Thus we drop the contingent nature of the world and its people and act as if it all really exists. We can act as if our consciousness is not an encapsulating room without door or window.

Insofar as economists, business folk, and all the other market and social technicians are of a given society, they go to similar schools which teach similar arts and science, theories and techniques. They adopt the same set of ideologies and indeed are virtual clones of each other. One would anticipate that the moral and aesthetic systems and values of such people would be similar. But insofar as the ideology of the society is *not* common but split among conservatives, liberals and radicals, and follows different analytic modes, value systems, and so on, one would expect analytic, ethical and moral differences. Furthermore if the operations of the world and its markets are smooth and orderly one would anticipate that the observers of the world would expect a continuance of such order. But let unruliness enter the world, its markets, its politics, its ideology, one would also expect the reflections about the world and its parts, and the future to be varied and even contradictory to the observers. People seem to be dedicated to finding order. So, many theories of behavior are developed.[1] The social and ideological differences among Americans, Israelis and Arabs are as significant as the national self interests of these societies in causing tensions. Nations may not have friends, but they have more than self interest to divide them. They have values and ideologies.

Thus in a calm world whose order is fairly undisturbed, and in an ideologically and educationally fairly homogeneous society of involved people, it is possible, indeed likely, that the theories about employment, income distribution, social values and responsibilities will exhibit rather small variances. But if the society and its markets are unruly due to externally caused shocks or whatever, and if ideology is not solidly fixed, one would expect the experiential and scientific structures to develop into competing and even conflicting explanations, forecasts, theories, and policies. This indeed has been the status of the world, including our Western

World since the Great Depression, since World War II, and perhaps since the industrial revolutions began.

The manager, in our language the prime mover in the firm, gets from his world all sorts of values and ideas of appropriate behavior. Among them are what is expected of him as firm manager as he makes decisions whose implications go beyond the immediate firm operations. Labor, buyers, sellers, competitors, shareholders, banks, many groups and persons will be affected by the managerial decision. The manager, by some mechanism of association, acceptance, rejection and organization, develops a mind set of what he believes is expected of him as manager.

Then a problem arises which cannot be handled in a rote manner. A free, novel choice has to be made in a situation which is different from others previously actually or vicariously experienced. What is expected of the manager then is not immediately nor simply related to what he will plan to do. The manager reflects, analyzes, has hunches or unexplained feeling about what to do. What is happening in the moral and technical sphere is a tension between what is perceived as the objective view of the world's evaluation of what to do and the manager's own, personal evaluation of what to do. The reduction of that tension by making a decision and acting we may define as an act of creativity or originality.

The technical content of the decision need not concern us here, although it obviously may be of very great importance to firm and manager. The ethical content is our concern. The manager's choices of behavior clearly are restricted by the technical means at hand. Ideally that would be the state of the analytic art and of the state of the technology. To go to such limits is usually not relevant. The issue may not justify spending much money on some new technology or consultative service. So the economic significance of the problem has more immediate limits. Then the manager, having marshalled more than one possible solution, if he is morally involved, must ask: "What are the internalities and externalities of the alternatives?" "What are the implications of this action?" That is to ask who will be affected and how, both within the firm and outside the firm by the alternative actions. This is an analytic problem, and unfortunately often the analytic tools at the manager's disposal, i.e. economic or social theory, are at best meager, while the issues often simply are not so great as to justify deep, detailed analysis. Failure, however, to undertake analysis can lead to embarrassment if some externality turns out to be significant e.g. air pollution or food additives.

Our point is that the manager, the responsible figure in the firm, is assumed to have resolved a tension of moral (and technical) values within himself. This tension is between what he thinks is expected of him, and what the immediate issue generates as to what he thinks he ought to (can) do. At one extreme he may walk away from the problem by resigning or passing it to some higher or lower authority. In either case he will not be a top manager for long if he avoids issues.[2] Obviously we have not faced the question of why a particular free choice was made rather than another. But we have narrowed the problem.

4 Ethics is Like Poetry

What a manager ultimately decides flows from his personal value system and his managerial style. But these, and the basis for his technical decision arise from his perception and understanding of the signals sent to him from the outside world. The technical and ethical values did not grow spontaneously. They are part of the order of the world, as he perceives and interprets it.

So there cannot be a personal or managerial ethic, in my view, which is not ultimately related to some social ethic perhaps only dimly perceived and interpreted in the particular, even unique experiences of a given manager. But business ethics, or better the ethics of business managers and the morality of the market, and I rather guess the ethics of any person, are the tensions within the manager (or other person), between what he believes is expected of him and what he, himself wants to do, ethically and otherwise. Ethical actions, which I take to be rather infrequent, are essentially self conscious in their essence. Such rare actions are deviations from perceived rules as laws and conventions. They are, in my view, determined by the experiences of particular time and place. For if a manager is *always* concerned with, let us say, labor's welfare or shareholder's interests, he is not, in each case making an ethical decision. He has made a commitment in the past and that is his rule. To *deviate* from this rule would imply an ethical choice, that is one specifically made given the conditions of time, place and exigency.

Rule by commitment is a reasonable, and in my view, an ethically valid way to manage. What is done in any case depends upon the case, but the implications of the available and chosen techniques and decisions follow a rule which, before it became a rule was an *ethical* decision.[3]

5 The Imposed Ethic – The Tension of Moral Imperialism

This leads us to the sticky question of what we might call Ethical Imperialism, a grand phrase for a fairly simple idea.

In most instances in business, the ethical act consists of transgressing a legal or conventional constraint by the manager. He uses the power of the firm so as to achieve some benefit for the firm as well as some benefit for the manager or other persons whose welfare, in the ordinary course of business, would not have been affected. In other words the benefit to the firm is accompanied by some benefits or disbenefits to non involved persons.

Ideally one should hope that the externalities are of a positive nature, benefitting those persons who, under the aegis of law and convention, may be involved. Practically more general benefits and disbenefits may flow from the action, and some may even have been planned.

The most flagrant type of negative effect charged to business is, I believe, unusually insignificant. Critics of the market, especially at the consumer level, often argue that a buyer (or seller) "took advantage" of the seller (or buyer). That is, ignorance and lack of power are taken advantage of to the *harm* of the trading partner. This kind of charge I believe, generally speaking, to be often exaggerated. The buyer (or seller) usually is under no obligation to deal with any given seller (or buyer), *even if the market is monopoloid*. Taking advantage of a trading partner is a short range advantage. Competition and substitutes are potent forces. If the seller is a legal monopoly (i.e. a public utility) the power of the state through its political system itself and the courts are also agencies of redress. Competition need not be kind to the individual.

In point of fact buyers from monopoloid (law breaking) sellers rarely use the tools of redress because they are costly, or because the benefits to be secured are not worth the costs. This is not a very desirable situation. But if the costs of monopoly are great to buyers, the aggrieved may act in concert via law suits, complaints and political action. The market is then forced into some reasonable structure by these non market forces. Ideally government, courts and the sense of market order and ideology on the part of sellers all operate to keep markets reasonably efficient and amenable to social values. Without seller acceptance of public amenity markets are doomed to replacement by some other allocative mechanism. In discontinuous markets e.g. bazaars of the Middle East, or in the spot contracting for crude oil or for other commodities, short run advantages may seem to occur as the short term market seeks its equilibrium.

Of more importance, I believe, is the circumstance in which a firm undertakes an action which it considers for the good of *some* party connected to the production process, regardless of other effects. For example a firm (i.e. the manager), which I once was observing, ran its cafeteria at a budgeted loss. This is, I think, not unusual. But what was strange was that the manager, in the instant case, the President, virtually dictated the daily menu, stressing certain foods. Upon inquiry from him, I learned that the President had strong opinions about diet (he was, in brief, a food nut on cheese and eggs). He was willing to use firm funds to make certain foods price appealing – for the good of the employees. I am convinced he was not very concerned with the relations between lunch and worker productivity. He *was* concerned with imposing employee welfare.

Other examples of such concerns of welfare are to be found in the arguments of managers on collective bargaining. It is not cynical to believe that many collective bargainers are sincere when they argue that higher wages, or increased labor costs will inevitably lead to unemployment increases. The sophisticated micro macro arguments and the equilibrial arguments are not, in the minds of the firm's bargainers meaningful or perhaps even known. The argument, as in the cafeteria one above, is simply that: "I, the manager, know your interest better than you do. So agree with me and don't complain when I act in your interest, against your convictions." Similar legitimation may be used to justify actions affecting consumers, suppliers, or even competitors.

This general kind of "do good" attitude, doing good in spite of the recipients' objections, is a kind of moral imperialism. The side with power imposes its will on the powerless, or at least less powerful. If the less powerful often see this moral imperialism as implicit in the market system they want the system changed. Very few argue in the direction of a less complex technology which would reduce the market power of the firm, most argue for either more government regulation or some kind of socialism (i.e. social ownership). It seems most likely to the present writer that moral imperialism, if it is a social evil, will not be solved by giving even more market power to a government agency or some syndicalistic organization. Other things being equal, the solution to moral imperialism, if it is a wrong, is to attack directly its excesses.

Moral imperialism may also be a characteristic of those in or out of the firm who require some particular behavior of the firm. The law is often not involved, for legal requirements are in a political and judicial sense requirements and constraints placed on *anyone* operating in the affected market. For example consumers of the firm's product may band together, agreeing to boycott the product so long as the firm does business in South Africa. Or reform agencies may try to force the firm to change its output or method of selling in certain markets e.g. Nestlé infant formula sales to underdeveloped countreis. After years of debate the reformers won. Another type of moral imperialism are attempts by politically active groups to secure funds for some cause from the firm, under the veiled or implied threat of political or market retaliation if the funds or other supports are not forthcoming. Boycotts are a major vehicle in such implied threats.

The subtle effects of advertising as imposing values is argued by Galbraith[4] and Hayek.[5] Galbraith sees people as sensitive to consciously directed forces which result in action which the observer may evaluate as irrational. Hayek disagrees. That values may be imposed on individuals and groups by others, seems to the present writer obvious.

Laws are often the imposition of a moral code on persons who would have acted contrary to the legal rule. Pollution control, minimum wages, product standards and honesty in advertising are examples. Law, however, is legitimated by legislatures and courts, non legally imposed rules may be onerous and harmful.

An overwhelming immorality, greater than any of moral imperialism, in a market however is for a manager, or several acting collusively, to depart from the legal or conventional norms of behavior motivated *only* by self interest. Such actions are with little or no regard for those who would be harmed and disadvantaged by the implications of the deviant behavior.

6 The Good and Bad of it All

Let is suffice here to note that firms i.e. managers, may plan to do good or ill, or may unconsciously do good or ill, to groups of people and individuals connected by some market nexus to the firm, or not so connected. The major consideration is that the power of the action of the firm (manager) is sufficient to affect people who have little say in whether they want the good done to and for them, and equally little say about being adversely affected by the firm's action. On a grander scale moral imperialism is exhibited when a developed country as the U.S., the Soviet Union, France or Great Britain undertakes some action, which is unilateral, to affect some less powerful country. The morality of the policy of the developed world toward the Third World is shot through with issues of moral imperialism. These are not very dissimilar from the related market issues we have alluded to.

Is there a general solution to the moral problems implicit in what we have called moral imperialism? Is it moral to seduce workers into a particular diet by manipulating prices in the cafeteria? Is it ethical to persuade employees to take lower wages on the theoretical belief that higher wages will limit employment? Is it justifiable, in short, to persuade (or force) anyone to act in a fashion which seemingly is contrary to his interests on the grounds that your knowledge and insight are better than his; that you are really doing him a good turn by protecting him against his ignorance?

The shoe may also be on the other foot. How moral is it to assure an employer that unless he pays a certain wage his sales will fall appreciably? Or to advise a company that unless it follows some particular, and in the mind of the manager, ill advised procedure, his reputation and that of his firm will be ruined or at least reduced in the public eye?

That such events occur in the real world is beyond question. Pressures, polite or legal blackmail, disagreeable and legally dubious choices are the experience of all who operate in the marketplace. How is one to judge whether the ends justify the means? That the ends never justify the means is an aphorism by which none of us live. The parent who assures the child being punished that "this hurts me more than it hurts you" is often, perhaps always indulging in a self justifying slogan which is meaningless. The kid is presumably being punished to correct some flaw in his behavior. The punishment should not hurt the parent, it should make him feel that he is somehow doing his duty. This deontological view is at the heart of the "Do unto others" moral creed. I do believe that such an approach of self-justification is, generally speaking, a little piece of self serving and moral rationalization which often is invalid.

But sometimes power may be, and indeed has been used to secure some moral goal. Other things being equal, an imposed or assisted decline in real wages may *well* cause an increase in employment. This generalization may be at the basis of a public policy which is concerned with *not* increasing unemployment generally. Controlling the diet, *via* price, of a work force *may* be beneficial to employees. Policies may or may not work.

Generalizations are dangerous. One must look to the particular event, to the specific circumstance, and be able to define the various benefits and disbenefits. Indeed the exercise of power in an arbitrary or capricious fashion, or the very existence of great power opposing little power, may be condemned as improper. Particular, relevant value systems of the society and the relevant value structure of management (or any power élite) become the crucial factors which create the social tensions whose release we consider the ethical act.

Fortunately the social system has provided a mechanism which solves many of the problems, ethical and otherwise, which are attendant of differences in power and persuasive ability. We of course refer to the law. If the manager bribes a labor spokesman, by one means or another, to acquiesce to some argument to the disadvantage of labor, then both manager and the labor spokesman are subject to severe penalties for collusive acts, and are immoral, in addition. If however the arrangements are unspoken and the benefits to the bribed bargainer difficult to detect, crime or at least moral deviation may still be present, but overt punishment may be absent. The law is not automatically effective. What courts call *"per se"* violations of equity e.g. conspiracy, supplying false information, or other criminal acts are illegal, but must be proved. Other acts which in some circumstances may be legal and in others illegal remain for courts to decide, provided someone brings an action. Firm A with 30% of the market merges or acquires firm B with 10%. Is the merger or acquisition legal? The court is likely to say a 40% control of the market is improper, especially if the remaining 50% is aleady concentrated among few firms. Share of market, and degree of concentration in American law are significant in the court's allowing merger and acquisitions. These are particulars.

In the hypothetical case cited above the question of legality or illegality of a merger or acquisition would be determined not so much by the exact wording of the anti trust statutes which are often vague, as by the court's interpretation. Such interpretation of law follows the Rule of Reason. The court's judgment in the particular case determines legality and illegality. Precedent, analysis, opinions of experts and ultimately the judgmental process of the court determines the issue. That the issue was and is considered to be significant rests on the statute which the legislature enacted because it had some moral and technical views on mergers. Not clear cut, well defined views, mind you, but some views that competition is a more desirable public policy than monopoly.

Some statutes have a sharper definition of the moral imperative than others. This is probably because some public issues have a sharply etched moral configuration in the public mind. Slavery is outlawed whether or not the slave is treated well or ill. Nor can a person contract validly to sell himself to slavery. Slavery simply is anathema.

A person however can, by contract, agree not to engage in a certain line of commerce in a certain market if he leaves the employment of a firm. This is an entirely different matter from slavery because the person is free to enter other lines of business activity than the proscribed one. The limitation may be a hardship but it is far from slavery. On the other side of the moral coin, a poorly educated, illiterate person may find the only job available to him is of such low pay that he cannot live on his wage. Slavery is not at issue, but welfare is. The legislature attempts to solve this problem by poor relief, free schooling, minimum wages, etc.

The legislature, then always has to wrestle with moral and technical problems in making laws.[6] Since neither the techniques for securing the ends are certain, nor the moral issues clearly defined and universally accepted, the courts have a job of work to do. The ethical component is intertwined with the judicial power. Courts, for example, have extended their concern to prisoners and very poor people who are, without protection. In this sense the courts have written humane concerns into the Constitution and into governance.

To make moral issues even more difficult than they otherwise are, *all* of such issues are not comprehended by law. Prior to the 1960s and 70s social revolution with its transvaluation of values, if revolution is not too strong a word, the rights of Blacks and other minorities, of woman and of the very poor were not so specifically guaranteed by legislation as they were after the 1960 reforms. Blacks, had the *right* to vote, women had the *right* to work, and handicapped children had the *right* to be educated, but little was done to implement such rights by substantive law. Public opinion, probably in most instances a minority white, middle class opinion, motivated legislative action. The result was that an enormous fund of social values was expressed as statutory requirement often without sufficient technical expertise to realize the fine statutory words by effective social action. The courts, too, were at a disadvantage, not knowing how to proceed. The general populace felt that specific legislation on more generally stated public action to alleviate some nagging problems, was required. Hence the state of regulatory statutes after 1964. The public, however, also found attempts to change social behavior costly, often unpleasant, with results which often were socially divisive. In short, implementing statutes based on less than available technical information and based on no agreed moral bases was socially disruptive.

The moral sensitivity of the 1960s, of Watergate and post Watergate, was reflected in the press, in public opinion and among members of the business society. The limits of the laws were very broad but not so broad as the limits of moral concern. Ideas of appropriate behavior became more sharply etched on the business and popular minds. The business conditions of the 1960s, 70s, and 80s however made business more chancy than in the 1940s and 50s, when business was, in general, highly successful. The ethical tensions of managers then became great. The election of Mr. Reagan probably acted to reduce somewhat the moral tensions. But morality still is in the business air.

As we noted earlier, the moral revolution of the 1960s which really began to be institutionalized in the late 1970s came at a time when morals and systems became the powerful tools of science, business, and government. The systems approach has affected the public generally. The public takes seriously the advertising about home computers, stereos, diet and gadgets as being "systems," i.e. self contained mechanisms. The idea has spread so that issues of women's rights, health delivery systems, minority rights and employment, ecological pollution, nuclear energy, etc. are all seen as parts of larger, more complex social and technical structures or systems. It is as if little can be neglected or passed over. Even small matters affect the larger whole, and the larger whole is often seen as vital to national or world well being. In our strident times nearly everything is taken, by some, to be vital to the society.

A remarkable reversal however has been in the rebirth of the traditional market ideology among business people and intellectuals, and a rebirth of political and social conservatism. In my opinion, the New Individualism which was in vogue late in the '70s and in the '80s is related to an unwillingness to pay the high taxes which reforms cost and to a less intense public concern with social minorities. That an ideal world did not quickly evolve is also a social criticism of what might well have become a better world.

The conservative trend has not yet stopped. Characteristic of the present has been to deny the moral and technical bases of many of the earlier reforms-affirmative action, special minority protection in jobs, educational benefits, health care for the poor and superannuated, an anti trust policy based less on structure than on performance. Entitlements and special protections are being eroded by ideals of economic efficiency. Thus the moral background of the United States is undergoing change, and with the social change comes a rethinking of the values of individuals, including business managers. A similar turning also is occurring in Great Britain, West Germany and elsewhere in Europe.

How long the social value structure will continue to move away from that of the immediate past, one cannot say. How private values will reflect the change, one cannot say. However if I were forced to make a guess as to the moral future, I should suggest that, in general, the values of the 1960s and 70s will persist, although becoming more adjusted to the technical capacity of the American and World societies to achieve the (vague) moral goals, and to pay the private and social costs.

It seems that there has been a shift in the concept of ethical market behavior. Not so long ago it was centered on industry's doing good. Now it seems centered on *not* doing bad. Ethics, in our defintion consists of actions which depart from required, conventional or self interest requirements. Departing from rule to do good is a fairly obvious exercise. Departing from rule to improve one's position or status is also fairly easy to understand. In the former case there is no injury, in the latter case, the person who breaks the law is subject to legal sanctions. If convention or market rules are broken, some other kinds of social sanctions are available.

7 The Law is Not an Ethic

How does one consider the sticking to the letter of the law, and by so doing reduce the welfare of others? Is this an unethical behavior? It surely is not, in ordinary circumstances, illegal. The laws and conventions of assuring pure air and water, the established rules of pure food and drug production, the controls on nuclear plants are not so effective as one would like. Is such lack of effectiveness conducive to unethical actions if knowledge and scientific signals indicate that danger is not reduced to zero or to a small probability by the law? The negative social consequences of sticking to rules without regard to how and on whom the disbenefits fall is probably of greater concern than issues of how industry should or might "do good".

Making the law vague, so as to include future knowledge or unprecedented behavior is a way, but not always a very effective way, to assure a minimum public exposure to harm. Using commissions as regulators, with broad powers has not altogether proved to be very effective. Restricting technical innovation is a sure road to stagnation. No single prescription seems adequate, so many are indicated.

Of even greater social concern is the feeling that managers, in the interest of their firms or of themselves, should stick to the book of rules, or only deviate from the rules by cunning. Cutting corners but obeying the rules in building a nuclear facility may yield some benefits to the company. But the possible dangers and costs to thousands of unsuspecting people who live in the general area of the plant are simply stupendous. A government agency's changing safety rules because of cost considerations, a charge sometimes heard, simply shares the unethic between builder and the government commission.

In its worst sense a positive unethic is an act which departs from rule or norm of behavior primarily in the interest of the actor. Sticking to the rule or norm of behavior when there is a high probability of untoward effects on non involved people is another of the currently discussed unethical acts charged to business.

The organizational structure of big business probably makes the charge of either type of unethic easier to make than for small business with its more informal structure. But because big business by its complexity is in a position to hide untoward acts, and shift responsibility, is not reason to assume that big business behaves less well than small business. Ethical abuses occur in markets with big and small firms, so far as one can see. Charges of holding illegal immigrants as slaves in the South and Southwest of the U.S. have been made against households and small farmers. The price conspiracy chicaneries of many small firms are well documented. On the other hand, when big business slips from the path of righteousness, its very size makes a slip seem like an earth slide. A bank failure which might have been averted touches the lives of many people. A nuclear explosion could be catastrophic. Impure drugs sold abroad may injure thousands. And so on. The very size of big business makes its lapses important.

It is the unethical or seemingly unethical lapses which have become more significant than ethical undertakings of business at the present time.

Footnotes

[1] J. Ortega y Gasset – *Concord and Liberty,* pp. 72ff., Norton, 1946.
[2] E. Schachtel – "Metamorphoses" in *The Psychology of Society,* p. 221ff, R. Sennett, ed., Vintage, 1977.
[3] L. Kohlberg – "The Cognitive Developmental Approach to Moral Education," Ibid., p. 227ff.

[4] J. K. Galbraith – "The Dependence Effect" from The *Affluent Society*, (Houghton Mifflin 1976) p. 240ff. in *Ethics of the Business System,* M. Missner (ed.), Alfred, 1980.
[5] F. V. Hayek, "The Non Sequiter of the 'Dependence Effect' ", Ibid. p. 246ff.
[6] J. Hurt – Ibid., *Law and Markets in U.S. History,* Wisconsin, 1982, p. 132ff.

Chapter V
Ethics – Politics – Practicality

1 Ideology as Values in Action

The Western World is not a world of unique ideology. Ideologies are, in our definition, social as well as personal values in action. How we behave as individuals, as nations, as a greater society, is a function of resources, technologies, history and self interest. Values, what must be done, what may or may not be done, what *should* or *should not* be done can be incorporated into the conception of self interest. To do so would dilute the conception and make it all things to all women and men. Self interest is best left only vaguely defined. It is the motive for maximizing benefits and minimizing costs or efforts. This definition is suggestive rather than sharp and clear.

We do not think that self interest, in itself, as a maximizing force actually exists or can exist in the marketplace. It is always clothed in the values, conventions and niceties of the age in which it operates. One maximizes income, if one ever really wants to, in the light of generally accepted constraints and restraints imposed by the society. For a business manager, self interest, meaning the interest of the firm possibly includes, in the 1980s, a concern with air or water pollution which was not considered in 1960 or even 1970. Public and private acceptance is, as a goal of business, logically prior to profits, sales and capital value perpetuity. And current acceptability often means a lively concern with pollution which first may affect other people in other areas, but quickly boomerangs to affect the polluting firm and its manager. If one manager restricts pollution, on his own volition, but no other manager does, then the general restraint is likely to be an ineffective tool. But if the pollution is great enough, law or other enforceable restrictions will ultimately be devised in an attempt to solve the problem. Is the action of firms, either taken singly or as a collective, to control pollution, a moral act or merely a piece of sound business? One cannot answer that question in the abstsract for it may, in the minds of the several managers have different meanings and answers. We can make the observation that pollution control is socially desirable, provided the social cost does not exceed the social benefits, and the techniques chosen are, all things considered, more effective than other techniques. But the measures are not all commonly agreed on.

The moral problem does not stop here. Pollution may be controlled, and at an effective cost, but the differential effects may act to change the distribution of income and power. Pollution may be controlled by introducing substitutes and devices which incidentally may reduce employment among some workers. Or the pollution control may provide windfall increases in land and property values which prior to the control were of low value, or the reverse may occur; previously high priced properties fall in value as previous non substitute properties now become substitutes. One can imagine all sorts of market reorganizations flowing from alternative programs of pollution control.

Pareto, the Italian conservative economist and sociologist, offered what has become, for some, an economic law based on total income maximization. If resources are optimally and equilibrially distributed, changing the distribution to benefit one person or group is only justified if the income of all or any is not reduced. To be sure an income recipient may make gifts to whom he will. That is his right in a free society. But to *require* an income transfer as *a cost* to other income recipients is to lower the total income produced, for the optimality and equilibrium of the maximizing condition would then be destroyed. The practical and political application of Pareto optimality was to make the implications of income maximization a moral imperative. Many economists, politicians and social critics, knowingly or unknowingly, have adopted Pareto's argument as a social ideal. If the maximization of income requires a competitive system come to equilibrial rest, it follows that any disturbance, *ceteris paribus,* must reduce the total. Distribution is not considered.[1]

2 Social Ontology

Nozick[2] the American political philosopher who makes the bizarre seem ordinary, is the philosophical equivalent of economist Milton Friedman in the current world. Efficiency, personal efficiency at that, is the controlling element in justice. Justice and ethics are generally treated as one. Justice is allowing one the use of the income which can be imputed to him or her. This, in effect is the marginal product theory of income imputation. Justice may well be concerned only with what Nozick calls "entitlements," but is ethics thereby ruled out? Entitlement to Nozick means the marginal product of effort, personal or *via* capital, if the operation and the preceding related operations were conducted freely, is achieved in a free, uncoerced society. Of course the distribution of income and wealth may be changed by a wealth holder or income recipient freely and willingly by transferring income and wealth to someone else. However to assume an uncoerced society does not mean that a society really can be "uncoerced" *in some sense.*

For Rawls[3], another influential American philosopher concerned with social morality, the marginal product income and wealth distribution in a free, uncoerced society also is in the nub of the justice argument. But Rawls argues that in a social setting the success (increased marginal product) of a person is related to the contributions of other persons. Then justice requires, in a free world, that if A's income rises then B to N's incomes also should rise because they are part of the general productive process.[4] In this argument Pareto optimality as an efficiency concept is amended by a justice concept which recognizes a degree of social synergy.

Rawls, like Nozick, is concerned with ethics as well as justice. First of all the theoretical underpinnings of Nozick's argument, assumes "holdings" i.e. assets of each person were *justly* achieved. But who can answer for the fair, just, or ethical acquisition of land or other property over the past 100 or 500 years? And what about fairness?

The Rawlsian incursion into welfare economics is enlightening. The simple utilitarian conception of the greatest good for the greatest number is exposed in its limitation by making it obvious that the greatest good argument is "indifferent to how a constant sum of benefits is distributed" (p. 77). Bentham's aphorism is a maximizing ideal not a distributive one. Rawls tells us that the marginal product of a dose of inputs is positive, but does not tell us exactly *how* to distribute the net addition to income or production. The functional distribution is not likely to be exactly just. However when discussing the basis of equality, Rawls suggests that the tendency toward equality is what one hopes for, and – "equality – is defined – as – mutual respect – owed to human beings as moral persons". This can be achieved if an increase in the income of A(dvantaged) also results in an increase in the income of D(isadvantaged). A and D are insolubly linked. *It is as if a just distribution of income tends to be a fair one,* i.e. the imputation of factor productivity and fairness, equality of the treatment of similar factors, are achieved by a dynamic adjustment of the distribution process. Rawls writes "a conception of justice is but one part of a moral view". This observation, in our view, also applies to Nozick and in general. It is the criticism of the neglect of a broader view of ethics which distinguishes our present approach from those of Nozick and Rawls, especially the former. Perhaps their concern is more political than market oriented.

Rawls and Nozick, especially the former, have had a strong influence on current economic thought, especially of the welfare variety. Analysis which stresses the duality, rationality and goods, have an automatic appeal for economists. The essentially libertarian cast of the two philosophers also has had a strong appeal. The view that liberty must, in a just society, be equally available to all is pure competitive doctrine. The view of Rawls that inequality is justified only when it has the greatest benefit for the least advantaged and if the less advantaged position is freely chosen, has a common sense ring about it. The Rawlsian idea of a social contract as being the product of some kind of consensus is subject to the same kind of attack which can be leveled against any social contract theory. Diversity of view, historical forces, conflicts of interest, and other heterogeneities mark most societies. Societies are dynamic, non equilibrial, historical products in which chance, history and ideas about the future all interact. Sahota[5] discusses the economic implications of both Nozick and Rawls in an instructive fashion. He gives the impression that the conceptual arguments of each does not provide much perceptual guidance to economic theorizing.

Our concern is centered on business ethics. Like Rawls, Nozick, and other political and economic theorists, I believe that it is economically just, as a matter of principle, to reward a person in proportion to his or her productive results. Incidentally, as Rawls seems to imply, exact measurements of productivity, marginal, average or total, for a person or unit of capital, are for all practical purposes impossible. What we measure is an approximation. Sometimes we know it is a poor approximation, as in the case of the similar earnings of a large number of employees on a fixed hourly wage, with differing qualities of skill, capital and supervision. In other circumstances the measures are a bit more accurate, e.g. in piece work. But at best, from any realistic view, given the nature of markets and plant operations, the per hour measures are only approximately accurate. Adjustments in wages, salaries and other payments, however, may be made in the light of ideas of fairness and justice. By and large bargaining brings about the adjustment. Law and convention which are based on some ideas of justice and fairness complete that exercise.

3 Market Ontology

The market, according to theory, is the process by which supplies and demands are equated. And it is a useful and explanatory theory. The forces of supply and demand are not, in reality, which is to say in experience, controlled or defined merely by considerations of economic efficiency. Supply, in price theory, is the hypothetical relations between cost and quantity offered expressed as a schedule. This is useful enough if one includes, as one should, all the obstacles to production which are imposed on the economic man and his market, i.e. minimum wages, social taxes, pure food restrictions, anti trust rules and so on endlessly. On the side of demand, simple utility and income are not enough. Buyers too, are restricted by law and custom as are sellers. Medicine requires a prescription, tools must be made so as to protect the user, buyers may buy cooperatively only after regulations are met, etc. And the non technical hindrances are not identical for all producers and buyers.

The regulations placed on the original economic man to make him a modern economic man are the result of the ideas of justice, public morality and fairness recognized by law and custom. These amenities, along with efficiencies, organize the markets in which the modern economic person buys and sells. Efficiency and amenity are linked. They interact so that the rules of the market change with the changes in efficiency as well as changes in amenity. New technology affects market structure not only by its immediate thrust, but also because it generates new amenities.[6] New values and ideologies affect the amenity ideals of the society and, in turn, call forth new technologies. To be sure sharp, cunning practices are practiced by some buyers and some sellers. These vary from the lawful to the illegal. But they are not the norm. Sharp practices are invasions on the integrity of any market system, and if general would destroy the system.

Amenities are rarely universally approved. They appear in law and convention as compromises. But new technologies too, are restrained and recast because of their cost effectiveness as well as the amenity structure. The cheapest technical way to generate electrical power is not necessarily the cheapest way in social reality. *Ethics is beyond market organization.*

But there is more to the distributive problem. The individual, the manager in our concern, makes contributions to the welfare of individuals and groups. He acts in his authority as manager of the firm. To some extent he justifies his actions as being somehow "good" for business and well they might be. For example hiring handicapped or providing scholarships to children of employess, when not required by law or convention, might be a thoughtful practice which makes the firm more socially acceptable than before. If so the action is a good business policy. But no one really knows when the exercise is first undertaken. The action might be simply a generous act by the firm *via* the manager. Then it must be judged by its implications, by externalities to determine its goodness and effectiveness. If the firm develops a policy of scholarships, then while the policy is being instituted, in effect, it has the spontaneity of the ethical act. An ethical issue however does not exist *after* the policy is in effect and institutionalized. Then the scholarship activity is based on a policy, or a convention, and loses part of its ethical flavor. Scholarships become a right or a perquisite, an entitlement!

4 Ethical Ontology

Ethics, as we define it, is an action *beyond* law and convention. It is a good freely willed act, and, as we have pointed out, to be judged as to its goodness by those involved and uninvolved. In our view a private ethic without a public ethic or span of ethics cannot exist. What a person plans ethically is measured against what he perceived to be the socially approved behavior at the time and circumstance. The resolution of the tension between the two is the ethical act. In its turn the act is judged publicly and privately by observers, interested and disinterested.

But what of the ethical decision by a manager, a freely willed decision to help someone or some group, say employees? The employees are told that the firm will give a bonus to employees who are not late for work during each week. Most employees are happy enough with the windfall. However the trade union may object on the grounds that the purpose of the bonus is to reduce the prestige of the union, and besides they weren't consulted. Other employees live a big distance from the plant, and have to take a ferry to get to work. The ferry, it is alleged, is late on foggy or windy days which are many. Thus these employees are not likely to even get the bonus, because lateness is usually due to foul weather. Rewards are based on where one lives!

Let us assume that the bonus idea was based on a desire of management to increase the income of employees, but to gain, at the same time, some fractional recompense by reducing lateness. In other words the motive of the employer was largely generosity.

Two considerations need concern us. *First* – If the bonus becomes institutionalized it becomes for all intents and purposes part of market structure and organization. Employees and the employer then consider it a convention, "ground rules" in the American vernacular, and any deviation unilaterally undertaken has ethical implications. *Second* – The bonus offer, made in good faith to all employees is considered a substantive intrusion by the employees who live far away. Their objection, possibly motivated by envy, can be overcome by withdrawing the offer, with all that such an action would entail, or allowing the objecting employees to resign. The trade union, if the action is not in violation of the contract, can only object and bring the matter up as a bargaining issue at the next collective bargaining meeting, or as a grievance.

The union matter is contractual rather than ethical. To a minority of labor the matter is ethical. Are the employees being pressured? Are their rights being violated? Such questions arise as ethical, and fundamental ethical issues.

Our reply in the instant case is that, continuing our assumptions of generosity, the manager has acted generously, if unwisely. He is, however, not coercing anyone. The objecting employees are not *required* to meet the bonus conditions, and if their envy is sufficiently painful they can quit their jobs or move their residences. The employer has no ethical obligation to adjust to their circumstance. It is possible that from the viewpoint of labor and contractual relations he might have acted differently to reduce lateness *and* do some good. Perhaps the two motives should have been separated. And perhaps the unions should have been informed and consulted with. But again this is a contractual, market matter.

Thus the ethical decision may have had some beneficial and some untoward results. We chose this less than earth shaking example to illustrate the complexity of analyzing the implications even of a minimal social act. The illustration also brings into focus the reliance that ethical decisions should have an analysis and reflection. The obvious but ineffective labor undertaking might have been ethically sound, but it would have been a mistake from the viewpoint of labor relations. Efficiency cannot be neglected as an intrinsic in production.

5 Market Efficiency for What?

In recent years, say since the 1950s, many economists have returned to the Smithean fold. Smith asserted that free markets tend to secure the best of all possible economic worlds. This is the invisible hand argument or faith which asserts that if each person is allowed to seek his or her own benefits in the market, what will be found is the best general social macro situation. The greatest economic good for the greatest number, the utilitarian ideal will be achieved in a sense, by letting Nature take its unimpeded course.

The analogy of markets to Nature, seems to underlay both the Smithean ideal of policy and the current ideology of many conservative economists and politicians. The Smithean ideal of policy is asserted rather than proved. It assumes that more goods are better than less, and that no producer or buyer is so large or important as to affect price by his or her actions. It also neglects the decreasing nature of average costs over a large range for many industries and firms. There are other assumptions, but the atomistic nature of competition is a necessary one. Then the motives of self interest should lead to ideal macro results, since the individual efforts would cancel out any extraordinary private benefits, with the result that the total social benefit would be achieved. Each person, by seeking to maximize his own benefit, would cause the totality of welfare to be maximized. Knowledge, competition and self interest are the keys.

The modern Smitheans argue in much the same fashion, although they do attempt to develop by logic and restrain by assumption what Smith believed by intuition, and by observing the behavior of state authority in less than free markets. Today the Saint George of Full Competition is again slaying the Dragon of Mercantilism. The moral and political legitimation of free markets is achieved through personal liberty or freedom. Liberty or freedom, however, is a complex public and private characteristic and amenable to many definitions and attributes.

Freedom or liberty is clearly a political and social conception as well as a market perception. To assert, as do some politicians and economists, that the outcome and output of any and all free markets (if indeed such markets could be operationally defined) are socially legitimated, however, does great violence to logic and experience.

In this regard, one of the standard conservative arguments is to assert that economic eminence and a morally justified political system depend on a "free" market economy. In effect it makes a good political system depend upon, and even require, a particular type of economic system. President Reagan praised the South Korean economic success of that nation, somehow assuming it approached a free market economy, but mildly suggested that placing political dissidents under house arrest during his visit was improper. There are at least two criticisms of Reagan's oratorical position. First, the South Korean economy is not a "free" economy in any accepted sense of that expression but rather is oligopolistic, with a kind of shot-gun marriage between industry and commerce on the one part, and the military on the other. Second, economic success, which is apparent, has not engendered a democratic political system.

American conservative academic economists, with some exceptions, are less professionally concerned with the economic and political linkages than are American conservative politicians. Economists seem to shy away from relating the subject of economics to the realities of politics. They are more inclined to discuss particular economic policies such as anti trust, or agricultural policy or wage regulation than to become involved in political philosophy, except in a general, unspecified, conversational way.

What interests most economists is market behavior, structure and outcomes. The market as a mechanism for converting resources to specific machines, products and services is the major subject of economics. Once this primary function is analyzed, then the distribution of income and of welfare are open to discussion, although economists often tend to see the economic system as value free. Now if a free market maximizes output, (which we hold is an assertion which has become an assumption) then particularly desired or considered acceptable income distributions, generally speaking, should not be sought by legislation lest it interfere with output. We should not interfere with the goose which lays the golden eggs. Welfare intervention should then be tentative, cautious and mild. In other words the goal of welfare is achieved, in such as system, by not talking about it too much nor too loudly; and not by making any market changes. Market amenities are out.

Such a view of economic and welfare problems, we suggest, is a Law of Nature view of society and markets. Markets, the assumption seems to be, should ultimately be based on freedom and individual liberty, with restraints to protect the liberty of everyone against the incursions of any one. (This caveat, however, can be the subject of all sorts of restrictions and requirements). The operation of this abstract, idealized society are, then, almost automatic. It is assumed to be activated by the motives of each actor, which are self interest and rationality. The whole is simply the sum of atomistic parts. Synergy, bias, unequal knowledge and capacity, all the realism is left out by abstraction.

The self interest theme has been used to a fare-thee-well in contemporary conservative political and social thought, although everyone *really* knows that motives are always, or at least almost always, diluted, utterly complex and inconstant. And markets, too, have other social purposes than the production of goods. As Harvard's Sumner Slichter observed half a century ago "Factories make people as well as goods."

In modern economic theoretical thinking by those whom we should classify as political and social conservatives, a class with more than its share of Young Fogies, the hypotheses of rational expectations and efficient markets are generally analytically relied on. The first hypothesis assumes that if a market intervention or regulation by government, or any other power élite for that matter, is imposed, rational behavior discounts (or adjusts for) the action and its results. Then the intervention or regulation will be frustrated by automatic atomistic corrective actions. Thus if the Federal Reserve gives a signal that it plans to increase the supply of money, those who would be adversely affected, immediately seek protection, possibly by buying bonds before the interest rate falls, or by putting off construction projects and capital investments, etc. depending on the expected concomitant rate of inflation. Increasing the supply of money will generate, the argument runs, one kind of "natural" price reaction if inflation is being experienced, another if prices are declining. Similarly households, foreign traders, and other groups will quickly discount the Fed policy, and so its goals will be frustrated. In a sense the rational expectation argument seems to suggest that often the effects of an economic action precede the cause. People act on rumor and expectation. Rational behavior sets up reactions before the policy can be implemented.

The actual situation and the expectations of the actors, however, are so varied that it is difficult to assume that a given policy necessarily has the same kind of effects in different circumstances. Nor is there often agreement as to what a policy or intervention implies for the economy or for an individual. Markets are not uniquely modeled by economists, business people or anyone else.

Similarly, rationality is at the heart of the second hypothesis, *viz.* the efficient market hypothesis. Indeed, the two explanatory hypotheses are blood relations. The efficient market argument asserts that self interest as a rational motive is so powerful that if an obstacle is placed in the market by some intervention, rational self interest will seek and usually find ways and means to overcome the obstacle. Thus if an income policy or any other market happening fixes wages and prices, sellers of goods and sellers of services will find ways to outwit the regulation which thwarts the rationality of the market. If wages are fixed, labor will bargain for and get *non* wage benefits or under the table benefits or fictitious promotions. If prices are fixed employers will cheapen the product or change the conditions of sale; while the buyers, because the regulation is requiring what we may consider "unnatural" terms, will shift to substitutes. In brief there is a reality, a natural mode of behavior, which will be realized in spite of attempts to thwart it in the name of some (wrongheaded) policy.

There is some obvious truth in both propositions-rational expectations and efficient markets, but the assumed truth is too general to provide a sound basis for a public policy which denies market intervention.

Both related hypotheses, rational expectations and market efficiency, depend we suggest, on at least three assumptions, and all three are jointly necessary although not sufficient. (1) The hypotheses view markets as natural phenomena rather than as artifacts or ideas. There is a "natural order" which markets follow, and interference therewith is at one's peril, or at the peril of all concerned. (2) Furthermore, the natural market is supposed to turn out results which are good for all, if not for each. (Pure profits tend toward zero is the conclusion.) The macro legitimation is social efficiency i.e. maximum product. (3) And finally, all actors on the scene have agreed on ways of assessing how the market works, what the results of regulation would be if allowed to work themselves out and also how one goes about avoiding and frustrating regulatory obstacles to the maximization of output.

Point by point, the three assumptions are not likely to be generally true, and the actions and expectations of actors not likely to be so coordinated and mutually supportive as is assumed.

1 Markets are social functions, processes, rather than things. The functions and processes have a history and the potential for change. Like the law, the election process, or any other social institution, there are elements of class or élite interest, fairness, historical uniqueness and general purpose, implicit in markets. They are not "natural" and governed by some benign constitution of markets. They are more parochial, and implicitly contain biases as well as elements of fairness and social efficiency. They are social institutions.

2 Markets may sometimes operate to maximize or optimize goals, or sometimes they may not. Regulations may be directed toward goals which have a purpose not contemplated by market participants, and may be rational. The first issue is "What is wanted?" Is it maximization or optimization for a particular good or service? Or is it some more general economic *and* social goal? How the product is made, how it is distrib-

uted, what is done with it are all issues which society imposes on and via markets. There are social as well as private issues, and no one element in the society makes the final decision.

3 Operators in markets differ among themselves (a) as to how the market will react to stimuli, (b) as to what is going to happen with or without external stimuli (exogenous variables or shocks) and (c) as what to do to protect one's investment or benefits.

In brief, theories of markets are many, and for each theory there are various micro theories of how to act to benefit one's position. Rationality is not a characteristic with unique attributes. Acting rationally may be quite different perceptions for different people. No one totally shares his vision of the future with any one else, nor do people generally share what should be done, even if they agree on the shape of the future. Finally, even if they happen to agree on what will be, and what to do about it, they may very well all be wrong.

So to assume:

1 that a desirable political system arises only or even mainly from the economic system is vague and usually incorrect,
2 that markets, by themselves, generate goods and services more effectively than markets encumbered by regulation is not very meaningful,
3 that all regulation (market intervention) is bad or good is wrong in the light of the complexity of goals sought.

Social theorizing must always be amended and justified by judgment and the particular state of affairs. To have an ideology is not to be an ideologue.

6 Legitimation as Rationalization

The rational justification of the state and government probably have little to do with the real, historical development of State and Government. But the rationalizations from Hobbes[7] through to Locke[8] and later all stress that government is the vehicle for protecting individuals from what might have been a "war of each against all" (Hobbes) or more positively stated, government is a mechanism which does for the individual, through organized action, what he could not do for himself. "Man's being–by nature free, equal and independent (cannot be placed in)–the political power of another without his consent which is done by agreeing with other men to join and unite into a community for their comfortable, safe and peaceable living, one amongst another, in a secure enjoyment of their properties, and a greater security against any that are not of it" (Locke).

Community (the society) and its formal operation (government) are supposed to improve the lives of individuals. For Locke, if not for Hobbes, individuals making up the social entity are sovereign. For Hobbes the Crown is literally the sovereign. But Locke, not Hobbes is usually seen as the philosophical father of Anglo-American rationalzation for the State and Government. The community through the art of government can do for people more than they can do for themselves. Individualism is the spirit of our political society.

Liberty, freedom and individualism, all three closely related, indeed so closely related *any* one of the three can be made to stand for the other two. This is a *sine qua non* of the Western social ideology. The shadings and variations of meaning may be slightly different for different commentators who look at what we may loosely call the Western-Democratic-Industrial society and for the different sub societies of that society. (The word "capitalism" is so differently used in the modern vocabulary that it is probably wise to avoid it. The same is true for socialism.) The essence of western society is that individual freedom, politically viewed, can increase the well-being, the welfare of the whole society, while protecting and securing interests (not all the interests) of each member of the society.

The last phrase is important, for the goal of society is *not* to maximize the entire welfare without any concern with individual welfares. *To make each one's life as good as it can be within certain restraints is a social welfare ideal.* An individual "in the market," cannot as a realistic goal, interfere with the social welfare as currently defined. To omit this caveat makes "the greatest good for the greatest number" argument a private ideal. Yet this ideal may have little or no concern with those who are of the society but not sufficiently in its production-distribution system, or who are, for one reason or another, not able to manage their economic lives. Maximizing total welfare is, politically and morally speaking, subject to the constraint that *the nature of the income or wealth distribution is also of certain shapes.*

From the market point of view, the individualistic concept requires competition if for no other reason than monopoly or oligopoly tend to exploit or neglect, economically if not politically, some members of society, and thus reduce their comfort, safety and peaceable living. The capacity of small enterprise to make a go of it against large enterprise would be slight unless the monopolist permitted the small firms to exist. This would reduce or deny the freedom to the small. Monopoly's regulation of the market or of general welfare is anathema.

Governance must limit market power of the powerful so as to make market structure acceptable to the generally accepted market ethics. Stated another way government must take steps to assure the tolerable existence of the small and weak. If this is not feasible, then some new concept of market must be developed. Markets are means not ends, tools not values. Thus the structuring of the market is not achieved by efficiency alone. Amenity is introduced by rule or law.

As time runs its course it is obviously clear that amenity, as an equalizing concept, has been expanded and amended to include not only the consideration of market competition, but also the notion of labor, consumer, seller, buyer, government, etc. Equalizing taxes are levied on firms in markets, rules are introduced, laws are passed, social restraints of a less formal sort are introduced, all as amenities. Efficiency in such circumstances no longer is the simple efficiency of costs and returns. The efficiency idea becomes complex requiring accountants, lawyers, economists and other experts and magicians in the art of market behavior to help the manager thread his way through what has become a maze of restraints and constraints.

What to do? This is a technical as well as ethical problem, a problem of justice and fairness as well as efficiency. No one really can expect an answer to this grave, political problem in any detail. At best one can only suggest a way out. In a word, the way out is Responsibility.

All actors on the social scene should assume responsibility for some accepted social ideology because their actions affect others. At the macro level resonsibility is part of the social ethic, of the social ideology. But responsibility is only a word unless it is buttressed by analysis, experience and an ideology which is in accord with the general principles of the society-liberty and amenity, – so that the principles of both and either are not violated. This is a vague prescription but useful enough to limit extreme measures. The resiliency of the market and social system may be counted on to correct minor violations.

Competition and democracy do work if they are not unduly restricted. Interest groups often try to better themselves politically and economically by seeking special advantage. Indeed if the business-democratic-industrial system fails it probably will do so because of the excesses of some interest groups which will probably justify their actions in the name of liberty!

At the market level the same prescription applies. Who will be affected and how, by some" engineered" change is the relevant ethical question. We say ethical, because all members of the market start out with the assumption that the laws and rules of the market should, as an imperative, be obeyed. If an individual manager morally cannot, he may drop out. If he tries to remain, then buyers, competitors and sellers will avoid trading with him. If he persists and disobeys the rules he is liable to the punishment of the law. If the law is immoral, the saving grace of democracy comes into play. He along with others may try to change the law. That is probably a major reason for democracy's success; it is viable.

The manager, no less than the employee, can always quit and do something else. This remedy realistically will only be used *in extremis*. But short of extreme circumstances change at the legistlative or administrative levels are possible. The freedom to quit a market or a job is clearly the saving grace of a market system, and the ethical safety hatch for the disenchanted.

At the individual level responsibility, again, is the implicit restriction on behavior. Because individual action is more visible at the level of the single manager does not deny its importance at the more complex levels of behavior. People act, institutions do not. Institutions are really figments of the imagination, and *persona ficta* are the reality in our world of "as if". People and firms act as if their motives and drives are known to us.

Thus education, private and public morality, art, science, decorous behavior especially of social and business leaders, and an implicit and explicit acceptance of the ideals of individualism, liberty and amenity are essential for a good society. The idelogies, myths, and legends of the society, through the various social institutions join in fashioning the private and public value system which include responsible behavior. Unless there is some ideological coherence the motives of behavior and the analyses of people would be disparate beyond words.

In our view ethics, a correlative of justice and fairness, is concerned with behavior which deviates from rule and custom. Ethical actions are freely willed and grow out of the tensions between the public and private conceptions of goodness. It is these conceptions which ultimately determine the ethic of the business manager. *Fortunately ethical considerations take up only a fraction of the time and energy of managers.* Active people are neither monkish recluses, philosophers nor logic choppers. Business managers are activists. How they act in the ethical, marginal cases are of importance to all of us.

7 Conclusion

We now are in a position to attempt a conclusion of our excursion into the market ethic.

1 The first proposition is not new, but it is basic. The society must be taken as a given rather than as some short term consensual arrangement. We are born into a society. We do not agree, *a priori* to act in concert with others. We act, in varying fashions, because society is where we are, and because we are what we are.

2 the second proposition is that the social contract, the rules of society are constantly written, rewritten, amended, interpreted, abused, and obeyed. Although society is logically and historically antecedant to any person or institution, its order and regulation are in constant flux due to new laws, ideologies and usages. These laws, ideologies and usages are, in effect, the social contract changes. Some changes are incremental, some, more rare, discontinuous. In other words society is not static nor only dynamic in the sense it seems to seek equilibrium. Society also changes with the new goals and new modes of behavior being not very well known or defined. The consensus back of law and convention are not unanimous. There are compromises and flat disagreements.

3 This proposition is that people depart from any one of the several acceptable norms of behavior for many reasons-technical, moral, out of ignorance or out of knowledge. Such departures from the norms of behavior may be the subject of social sanctions if some social or private disbenefit occurs. The assumption is that the departure usually involves some idea or hope of benefit to the actor. Self interest is a motive. Ethics is not yet involved.

4 The self interest motive, however may be strong or weak, or in the case of saintly actors, non existent. But to some extent, greater or less, there are in ethical actions desires and motive to benefit others, and the belief that the actor's departure from the norm will do so. Self interest is the counterweight of generous behavior, and the mix of self interest and generosity is not constant in differing situations. Insofar as generosity is the greater, the ethical component is greater. Insofar as self interest is greater, the ethical component is less.

Thus if a manager undertakes a cost for the firm by giving scholarships to children of employees, his behavior may or may not be ethical. If the grant is for improving public relations or assuring a smaller labor turnover, or greater skill in employees, the action is instrumental but not unethical. The program is in the self interest of manager and firm. But if the manager, recognizing the P.R. factor, sees it as small, and goes ahead with the project because he wants, at a cost to the firm, to better the futures of families of employees, the action is ethical. The norm of behavior is departed from, at a cost, in a disinterested fashion, to help others.

To be sure the manager may be wrong in that the education is put to no use; or his shareholders may object. As the program settles down and becomes a norm of expectation, it loses its spontaneous, ethical tone.

Should the manager have developed a program which, by grants and gifts, developed untoward habits in the work force, because of the malevolence of the manager, the act would be considered unethical. Such planned malevolence, fortunately, is rare.

What if the manager made a disinterested gift to the P.L.O. or to political terrorists? He and the firm had nothing to gain. However let us assume that the manager had a romantic sympathy for the objects of his generosity. One might, by our analysis, consider the gift a generous and an ethical one. Others in the society might find it unethical. But the spontaneous, freely willed gift was a departure from the norm of behavior, and with little self interest involved. Therefore it is in what we may call an ethical range. The questions of the wisdom and the implications of an ethical act are not resolved by calling it ethical. Points of view and values of the actors, observers, and those affected are all relevant in an ethical evaluation. There are many value systems with satisfying acceptability.

5 Thus ethical acts are costly to the actor, motivated by ideas of generosity, small in self interest content and above all freely willed departures from the usual, normal modes of behavior. They are walking the extra mile and more than sharing the cloak. Also, and probably fortunately, they are rare in the market economy.

We cannot avoid stewing over the aphorism of Franklin's "Honesty is the best policy".

Footnotes

[1] A. Schumpeter – *History of Economic Analysis,* p. 858ff, Oxford, 1954.
[2] R. Nozick – Anarchy State and Utopia, Basic Books, 1974.
[3] J. Rawls – *A Theory of Social Justice,* Harvard, 1971.

4 Ibid, "The Tendency to Equality," p. 100ff.
5 G. Sahota – "Theories of Personal Income Distribution." *J. Economic Literature,* Vol. XVI 1, p. 27ff.
6 Schumpeter, Op. Cit., p. 14ff.
7 T. Hobbes – *The Leviathan* (See Ch. 6), Oxford, 1967.
8 J. Locke – *Second Treatise on Government,* (See Ch. 2), McMillan, 1956.

Part II

Chapter VI
Market Ethics as Market Failure

1 Why Theory? Why Ethics?

One important general purpose of any discipline is to find or suggest some order in the phenomena being considered. Thus the observer must stand ready (1) to change his or her conceptions of meaningful, hence appropriate, ways to examine a reality, – a part of the external world and (2) to posit new and different conceptions of reality, hence of the *nature* of the external world. As (2) develops (1) is thereby amended and reconsidered. It is apparent that both observed and observer are caught up on the same exercise. The purpose of the exercise is to assert some order and orderliness in the phenomena being studied so that other observers using the same or similar analytic and ontological assumptions will also find the order.

A theory or generalized statement, then, legitimates the discipline, or at least a school of thought, because it can be asserted that the theory is in accord with the reality of Nature. To be sure Nature is rarely so persistent that it operates only in completely defined and precise limits. Variations of behavior occur and often, in the social disciplines, theory, seems to be a bad fit for what is observed. But the bad fit can partly be explained by the accidents, the exogenous forces which intrude themselves but are not really a necessary nor implict part of the phenomenon.

Price, for example, may be generally related to income and tastes, but neither are absolutely fixed in the short or long run. Changing technology, advertising techniques, and tastes may intrude and change the original relationship, which was assumed to be free of accidents and exogenous forces. Reality does not stand still for any one.

But price may be analyzed in other ways than by any one particular market assumption. Price may be analyzed in terms of the long run, or short run costs, average or marginal, substitution costs, and so on.

The demand and the supply sides may also be joined to create a hypothesis more complex than the previous cases. In economics the so called neoclassical synthesis which purports to marry micro and macro equilibrium analysis, is such as attempt on a grand scale. Sadly, as theory grows more complex and all encompassing, the role of historical accidents and exogenous variables become more obvious in the phenomena being examined. Then the original assumptions or assumed set of variables seem insufficient to explain a complex phenomenon. Endogenous and implicit assumptions evoke exogenous and explicit variables to become part of the theory mechanism. What seems inside the system sometimes depends on outside forces which were not assumed to be in the system at all. Monetary policy at the national level or sales policy at the firm level never quite work out as anticipated. Unexpected data or absence of data almost always get in the way.

Persistence of order and regularity in the limited world being theorized test the theory. The theory therefore legitimates itself. In truth theory does *not* explain anything, it merely records what has happened, and hopefully, what can be expected to happen as one observes a stripped down, simplified phenomenon. As beauty is its own excuse for being, so is social theory. When we say theory "works" or "explains" we mean that in a loose fitting fashion the ideas of observers can be made to match or fit the observations. But one should always remember that:

1 If one theory can be made to fit, other theories, too, can be made to fit. This can be accomplished by approaching the phenomena to be studied from different viewpoints e.g. (1) price in its context of price to consumers vs. (2) price in its context of cost to producers vs. (3) price in its more synthetic aspect of supply and demand.
2 The observer and the phenomena being observed are intimately related. The observer adjusts his viewpoint or calls on apperceptive resources to clarifly the changes in the thing being observed; and what is observed reflect, in part, the apperceptions of the observer.

Slavery, for example, as an issue in American life provides an interesting case because many sets of propositions, ethical and legal, have been offered to explain and legitimate the institution.

A little over 100 years ago there were people who argued that slavery as a property institution had a legal legitimation (which it did) as well as a moral legitimation *from the viewpoint of the slave*. The certainty of the slaves' care and feeding, the built-in social security, the slaves' psychological indifference to freedom, plus fear of its implications, indifference to familial affection, etc., were built into a set of propositions which might be called The Good Theory of Slavery, or The Theory of Good Slavery. The institution then, minus exogenous factors, was an "explained" phenomenon within the parameters of law and a revealed ethics. The theory therefore "explained" the institution and was legitimated in the light of law and ethics.

Needless to say there were those who argued that slavery was unethical in the light of another set of ethical and analytical propositions (apperceptions). This view attacked the moral legitimation of the law and the validity, hence legitimacy, of the freedom attitudes, values, hopes and desires of slaves. Furthermore what the opposition considered social exogenous factors e.g. the ill treatment of slaves by the observed standards, were not accidents at all, but implicit in slavery. This is the "Uncle Tom's Cabin" approach. It, supported by the accidents of politics, social and economic development, led to a bloody civil war and to the abolition of slavery as an institutional and legal form in the U.S. But, sad to say, as was inevitable, the abolition of slavery, as a legal form, did not eradicate *social* and *political* issues arising from the abolition.

That the open sores as well as the scars of slavery persist cannot be denied. No one argues for a return to slavery as a solution for race issues. Whether or not slavery was efficient economically is beside the point. It was a social evil. The issues now revolve about the status of Blacks in the society. In this brief discussion of slavery we have viewed it as an institution. Today it is an institution which has outlived its legitimations, moral and legal. What once was a divisive issue no longer is even arguable.

In today's world the transfer from economic or economic-efficiency legitimation to a more general social legitimation also occurs. The creation of a public deficit is legitimated if it puts to work people and resources which otherwise would not be used. Or it is a way of reducing current taxes if they are perceived as too high.

The point is that theory is used to legitimate a course of action, and theory itself is legitimated if it explains or predicts what it purports to explain or predict.

2 Means and Ends

Even though the world, the external reality, is considered a continuum, it is customary to divide it into many universes of discourse. Herein we often err because what is impounded as being constant may not, in fact, be constant. The speculative builder, the portfolio manager or the family saving against a child's university education, cannot exclude the consideration of long term interest rates from the planning process any more than a city planner can neglect demography or industrial migration. And such elements are subject to change. The world is a continuum whose parts adjust and interact in persistent as well as extraordinary fashions.

In spite of such continuity, for practical purposes we distinguish between means and ends, largely or usually on a time basis. What comes before is the means to what is emerging. And once emerged, an event, an end, is a means to some other end. Ends, however, sometimes occur *before* the immediate means. This is implicit in efficient market arguments. Consideration of a money policy may produce results before the implementation of the consideration is put into place.

All this may be a bit tedious to the reader, but we are trying to set a stage for a discussion of ethics.

We define an ethical act as freely willed, costly to the doer in some sense and undertaken to benefit another person or persons. (Benefits may be a disbenefit which makes the act a negative ethic, or evil.) But how the benefit will be used, for good or evil, is in the future. A costless act which benefits a second party is, in our view, not ethical. Cost may be viewed as an opportunity cost.

If an employer freely gives scholarships to the children of his employees, such an employer is a good man or woman. The gift is assumed to be without any or with minimal self interest. The assumption is that education is a good. It is, usually, but not always. Some educated people are supposed to be less happy than dolts; some educated people become swindlers or con artists, or even revolutionaries. But this is trivial. The goals of ethical behavior *generally* are socially legitimated. Ethics is generally a means concept, an action undertaking, with expected immediate goals of benefit i.e. socially and personally normative.

Therefore a freely willed act may be dangerous and even morally reprehensible if undertaken without a careful analysis and reflection of its possible and probable implications. The failure of analysis and reflection may render the undertaking not only deficient but a hardship and misadventure for the recipient of the gift, and for others who are adversely affected. Hell *is* paved with good intentions.

In a sense then, the ethical act is to give someone something he or she did not *buy*. It is not a market transaction of exchange since there was supply but no demand in the traditional meaning. The gift then represents a species of market failure. The wish for, or want of, is not effective demand.

We define market failure as the giving or getting of some scarce utility (or disutility) without a counter, freely undertaken giving or getting. No market exchange has taken place. If a firm (unethically) dumps waste into a river, the firm is divesting itself of noxious waste and giving it to the downstream users of the river. The recipients have an unwanted gift, which turns out to be costly. On the other hand, a firm may (without legal requirement) neutralize the waste before dumping it, and in neutralizing it so change its chemical properties that the dirty water of the river is cleansed! Again a case of market failure, but one which is welcome to the down river populace. The action (or chemical overreaction) is an ethical act quite regardless of what the downstream people do with the water.

Law, too may be looked at as a special of market failure. Legislators make laws. There is no formal market exchange, there is a political exchange with the ultimate recipients the citizens, in the short run, having no recourse. A failure of law can later be corrected by repeal of the law or by voting the rascals out of power and voting in a new set of legislators.

Any action between two bargainers *not* of approximately similar economic and social status; in short any exchange action outside a *competitive* market, implies some kind of transfer of utility (or disutility) between groups or individuals of *unequal* bargaining status. The mechanism which controls the utility exchange does not function effectively hence the market has to some extent failed.

Ethics then is an action outside the (competitive) market. It is a corrective to disutility or unfairness or unjustice generated in the market. But ethics is outside the competitive market mechanism. The recipient is passive and at the end of this exchange process. To the extent that a monopolist or oligopolist uses market power for self interest, to that extent there is an ethical implication of market failure, for market failure may be extended to all non competitive transactions.

Justice and fairness in a market are generally assumed as desired outcomes of ordinary and traditional (competitive) market operations. Indeed interventions by law and rule are introduced into traditional markets with their varying degrees of non competitiveness with the idea of securing justice and fairness. Such purposes are the ultimate legitimation of all market intervention, whether or not the interventions, in fact, are effective. Justice, in a crude and approximate sense, is attained by arrangements which purport to award each actor in the market a reward equal to his or her productivity. This is the moral legitimation of the marginal productivity theory of income distribution. Justice in the market however is an approximation because productivity is difficult to assess.

Fairness is a corrective to this crude imputation doctrine, crude because who knows exactly what share of the product any individual or group should be entitled to receive? Fairness is ultimately a statement that morality requires that similarly situated people should be similarly rewarded and treated; and furthermore that rewards should be somehow related to need. The idea of situational comparison is often the subject of controversy.

Men and women doing the same work once received unequal pay since men, in general, were supposed to have greater financial responsibilities than women because men were heads of households. The opposite might just as easily have been argued. Women work because their families keenly need their income, therefore women probably should, as a moral matter, be better rewarded than men. Their needs are greater. In some European countries family allowances based on the number of children in the family are made to employees in addition to their wages.

Fairness is a corrective for failure to achieve justice or because justice is not an appropriate measure. Fairness is hard to come by as the people involved become more different in their social and market behavior. But how to compare the productiveness or needs of a school teacher and an electrician?

The capacity of markets to determine and assure market justice and fairness in a fashion acceptable to a society is limited. Therefore nonmarket correctives are needed, if social harmony and ideology are to be satisfied. Some occur within the general market system, some are outside the market. Within the market income transfers, as in Social Security, veterans benefits, tax credits for interest payments, and various tax loopholes are examples. Outside the market free public schools, costless radio and television programs, police and fire services, and Medicaid are examples of ex market correctives. Such regulations are designed to assure some amenity in the market.

To be sure public actions are often related to market reactions, since taxes paid or avoided link the market to the nonmarket; and public services privately provided have a way of entering costs and prices. Costs and returns are ever present in social and private arrangements, and many costs and returns are measured in money, which is a market yardstick. We recognize both the continuity of the real world, and that arbitrary divisions in the continuity of reality are made for analytic purposes. The world is too big to be grasped as a unity. It *is* a unity, but to make analysis possible we break it down (at our risk).

Thus the ethical ideal or ideals, which are the ideological aspects of justice and fairness permeate the society, in its market and non market aspects. The ideal of morality – of ethics – permeates every aspect of the society. But ethics implying not a free exchange but rather a freely willed, unilateral action, is essentially outside the market.

3 Market Ethics, Justice and Fairness

Markets are primarily institutions of exchange. But all institutions involve, to a greater or lesser degree some aspect of exchange. In a market there is *always* the exchange of utilities. Goods and services are bought, sold, leased or otherwise exchange for a price, for something of market value. Such exchange enables both parties, buyer and seller, to go about his or her business with some newly acquired economic instrument making him or her feel as if the exchange involved some advantage. To this extent there *is* a free lunch, in spite of all the sage Friedmanite scorn of the idea.

In production we attempt to join land, labor, capital and entrepreneurship so that the sum of the values of the inputs is exceeded by the value of the output. Such economic, productive synergy makes an economic system possible. The family, state, church, military, art, exercise, any and all successful undertaking and institutions produce or are expected to produce more value that it takes to operate them. The market is no exception. The problem is to define and measure the values of the inputs and outputs. This cannot always, even usually be done in money measures, probably even for markets.

Now, except for markets, exchange measured in money is, generally speaking, anathema, crime or some other untoward and low epithet. The modern world is a world of rules, and among the rules is that markets, generally speaking, should be the major scene in which money talks.

Legally or socially rules restrain and constrain. Thou shalt pay equal wages for equal work is a legal constraint. Thou shalt not employ children under 16 years of age under certain conditions is a legal restraint. Such rules are wont to interfere with the engineering and (pure) economic conception of efficiency. In brief economic efficiency as a minimization of, input value per unit of output value is not an absolute concept, but is constrained by non economic considerations. The maximization of output value per unit of input value, too, is a constrained maximization at best. Amenity – social requirement – is ever present; and, other things being equal, tends to grow as the wealth and income of the society grows. It is as much a mark of modern civilization as technology.

As society grows more complex, as markets become larger, as technology becomes more intricate and its wheels encompass other wheels, rules replace decisions which formerly were, at once, ethically derived and technically oriented. Particular circumstances once evoked managerial reaction to each circumstance. Now more general, hypothetical predicaments are addressed by rule, so administration often is of great importance in a problem. In large scale industry and trade, reliance on rule is required by organizational size and complexity. But as strict rule isn't always relevant it is often made less strict, more relevant and potentially dangerous, one might add, by being somewhat loosely defined to include administrative discretion.

Trading partners, both suppliers and buyers, are sometimes linked by written contracts but often only by oral and situational connections. The consumer trading partner who buys a loaf of bread or one who sells his or her products to a firm, usually relies on a spoken offer and acceptance. Such arrangements permit buyer and seller to withdraw easily from future contracts with the firm if the arrangements are unpleasant or disadvantageous. Competition is a great inducement to appropriate, reasonable and friendly, i.e. ethical behavior on the part of both buyer and seller.

Monopoly and the other degrees of imperfection of market competition provide the opportunity for untoward, hurtful behavior. Hence the reliance on competition as an ideal in the law and economic theory. Competition is not an ethically free concept. Evil is impossible, it is held by enthusiasts of competition, for long, at least in a free market, while goodness is always possible. But market complexity and inequality of market power among the several bargaining parties induce government to step in to restrain evil and constrain the contending parties.

4 Regulation as an Old Dodge

Market regulation did not begin with the New Deal. The regulation of markets is about as old as bargaining itself. The ideal of free markets – laissez faire – as an ideal is scarcely three centuries old, as a total practice it has no age at all. However, the determination of which groups in the market system deserve and require government assistance, and the goals and means of such market intervening assistance change from time to time. Price fixing, the abolition of slavery, the so-called sanctity of contracts, non contractual activities, restraints on contracts, specific performance, liability, and so on endlessly, are and have been the substantive content of law, regulation and administration since exchange as a formal institution has existed.

Presumably exchange benefits both parties or it would not have occurred. A required exchange or one under duress is no market exchange but a species of coercian and compulsion. The robber who says "your money or your life" while pointing a gun at his victim, is not a market phenomenon. Bargaining with terrorists only *seems* like a market phenomenon. There is no stability in the arrangements. Nor is the public utility which supplies perhaps more services than one wants, but at a higher price than one considers fair, a purely market phenomenon. Extra legal violence is a threat to appropriate behavior. Public utility pricing, not a competitive phenomenon, is a governmentally controlled and sanctioned institution. Both differ from competitive market institutions.

Governmentally regulated institutions or even more essentially other non market institutions as the military, the legislative, the administrative, the family, educational bodies, jails, and other social forms in Whitmanesque profusion also tend to have elements of exchange – utility exchange – among their functions. Families exchange care for affection as well as out of duty, and so on. Educational institutions exchange teaching, knowledge, research, and services for the cooperation of students, their attention, and *inter alia* for government and private funds. Even jails exchange custodial care, feeding and ideally some correctional efforts for prisoners' behavior and cooperation and for social protection. None of the institutions perform with the excellence and effectiveness that the whole society or any member would like. Nor are the exchanges – coerced, required, necessitated or even voluntary, – the same as the *quid pro quo* of a free, competitive market.

The child, the convict or other beneficiary of non contractual care cannot

121

freely and voluntarily quit the institution in which he or she is. The student or the buyer of electricity cannot simply and conveniently change his or her trading partner. How awkward it is for a court to assess damages in a civil case of wrongful death or injury. The driver of the car did not plan nor want to injure the pedestrian. It was an accident pure and simple. Yet it is treated as an exchange and a price exacted. The underlying legitimation of the non market institutions is not simply the same as the legitimating ideal of the pure and perfect market.

The market, in its turn, however, borrows legitimating ideals from the other institutions. Ideas like the vested rights of the labor market, or rights of the child have a place in social institutions. But analogous ideals also have found their way into markets. Working people cannot be laid off because a manager is biased against people of color (as a child cannot be discarded because the parents wanted a girl and got a boy). And firms are required to pay people performing identical work identically.

To assert that *ideas* are tested in the *market* of ideas, is to imply that if the offer and acceptance of an idea are consumated, the idea is a good one because a sale has been made. Offering and accepting knowledge which is in error, factual or analytic, does not make the flawed knowledge correct. This is one of the great weaknesses of political democracy. Political debates suffer so often from the ill informed convincing the ignorant. Truth should be involved.

One might surmise that the *quid pro quo* arrangements of the market are more easily, and probably more successfully, regulated by the amenity intrusions of custom and regulation than is the case in other institutions. Families, with their inherent privacy; politics with its myriad of interest group pressures; the military with its fatal mystique; science with its veil of hard to pierce epistemology and methodology and the reverence which our time extends to science; religion with its transcendental method of communication and sacred rituals are not easy targets for regulation and reform from the outside. Markets on the other hand are accessible and secular. Man may not live by bread alone, but getting by without the metaphorical bread bought in a store, would be an horrendous experience.

The regulation of markets to assure amenities is an attempt to secure justice and fairness. How well the popular, political, aesthetic and moral efforts succeed depends, of course, on technology, resources, the administrative skill of the managers of the society, as well as on the conception of justice and fairness which have been adopted. Insofar as the regulations succeed and the output is not unduly diminished, the market function is legitimated.

But justice and fairness, even if attained in the market to the satisfaction of legislator or idealogy do not always satisfy participants in the market. Some want more, some want to give more or less. Those wanting more seek their ends by attempting further regulation of the market e.g. by trade union organization, training programs, income transfers, etc. Those wanting to give or get more or less can achieve their ends by simply transferring income outside the market mechanism using taxes, subsidies or gifts.

In the economic sense markets are processes of exchange in which goods and services are traded for money prices. In competitive markets control over price and quantity are out of the power of either buyers or sellers. There are degrees of competition, so that as competition grows less, the market power concentrated in some buyers or sellers increases. As the degree of competition increases, that is the concentration of market power in the hands of fewer buyers and sellers decreasees, the opportunity and probably desire of buyers or sellers to introduce other values than price into the equation of exchange diminishes. To the degree market power increases, opportunities for imposing *non market* values, good or bad, increase. Thus the public and private fiscal systems play roles in welfare via their effects on income distribution.

In non economic exchange, non market – non price – motives are stronger than in market situations. Ethics, therefore, are not part of the economic activity, but rather are part of the *setting* of exchange in market situations. It may be part of the essence of exchange in non economic activity.

Chapter VII
Law and Economics as Legitimators

1 Reality as Assumption

Insight is seeing new relations among the parts or elements of a system. The systemic complex of parts, in its turn, is seen in some functional manner. Systems have purpose as well as mechanical interrelation. Airplanes fly, razors shave, even boondoggles amuse kids and keep them quiet.

Insight is a species of theoretical or abstract grasping of a functional unity which is *not* based on past experience. Rather it ascribes a function, hence purpose, to a process which has not been rationalized by the observer from his/her immediate or vicarious experience. The miracle of penicillin is that Dr. Waksmann had the insight to grasp the significance of an unknown relation between a mold and an infection.

Hence insight is related to intuition, to innate ideas, or even to some transcendental force. If the insights are limited, that is do not deal with grandiose ideas as life, goodness or universal truth, they tend to be harmonious with other processes which experience has, in a way, validated. Such experience tested insights are the substance of knowledge in its many forms, knowledge which can be discussed by people who, too, have participated in similar experiences.

Uncertainty comes when the experience of insight cannot easily be communicated and discussed. Then the insight is transmitted to faith, and its communication based mainly on persuasion. Not that this inhibits discussion and communication. Artistic, aesthetic, spiritual, ideological and other conceptual entities which do not rely on generally accessible perceptions and ideas are universally the subject of conversation, discussion, dispute, argument and controversy. Being reduced to some experiential base only with difficulty or not at all, such insights and insightful experiences cannot often, or perhaps ever, be fitted into a system based on experience and reason. Politics would become mere technique if everyone agreed on social problems and their solution.

The greater the insight and its implications, the more likely the reliance on intuition. Therefore the greater is the difficulty of communication – of explaining on the one part, and understanding on the other. Transcendental assertions are to a great extent communications about what cannot be communicated. That aesthetics, ideology, spiritual values do provide the bases for group beliefs and behavior is a rare tribute to the capacity of people to exercise imagination and, in a sense, will themselves into the state of mind and experience of other people. When brute fact, experience, disequilibrium, or the disharmonious state of the supposed "system" denies the validity of the insight, problems arise for the faithful.[1]

If the transcendental system is a large one, say encompassing morality, life everlasting prosperity, peace or national honor, its dysfunction may engender social and psychological stress of great moment. Watergate and its aftermath which involved national honor surely had serious and baleful effects on America's self image. The inflation of the late 70s and early 80s affected more than prices, it also affected the American and European faith in the American economy. The Reverend Jesse Jackson's race for the Democaratic presidential nomination in 1984 and 1988 has affected and will continue to affect the political and social ideology of whites, Blacks and other minorities. The hostage crisis in both Iran and Lebanon had and will have repercussions far beyond the time and persons of the happening.

Our point is that the inner, innate goodness and harmony of a political, economic or other social system is more assumed, posited and accepted as a matter of faith than as a verifiable experience. Such strained systems, as part of a larger ongoing system, operate along with other subsystems; and all interact.

The family exists and operates in a political system, with many contacts between them. The money and banking system can be alternatively viewed as part of the economic system, or as a system of its own which is closely connected to the system of production and income distribution. Both views, the integrated and the dual have their advocates, and for differing analytic and policy purposes each may be a correct and useful view. How Federal Reserve's real assets are taxed, an issue of a generation ago, had little bearing on the money supply for the U.S. The tensions were contained. Similarly political reform or control of drunken driving or voter registration or even social security have had minimal effect on the U.S. – Soviet relations or U.S.-Latin American policy. On the other hand U.S.-International Monetary Found relations might have a great effect on American bank liquidity and on developing countries political and social stability. Bank policy through employment, output and expectation affects family stability and University budgets.

Once a system is envisioned, it often can be reduced to a number of subsystems whose analyses are sometimes called disciplines. They are related for some purposes, unrelated for others, and integrated for other purposes. Medicine with its specialties, and economics with its breakdowns are cases in point with respect to disciplines. And the disciplines are justified insofar as they are concerned with some definable system delimited for some purposes. Reality, the interrelations of experience, is an ephemeral experience itself which cannot be ultimately defined. It is only partial. The relations among the parts of this system or process are inferred rather than exactly known.

At best what we consider reality is partial, inconstant, and emerging. At worst reality is part of the experience of an observer who sees a thing or event as isolated and unconnected. Wishful thinking is ascribing a reality to what one wants to believe although it has no validity. It is an opposite of insight.

2 Two Analytic Tools

To bring the discussion down to a more operational level we shall focus on the market as the reality and on economics and the law as the analytic tools.

Interesting questions turn on the issues of what kind of tools, that is to say assumptions, shall we use to explain market behavior. The total equilibrium assumption of some macro economic models, the partial equilibrial assumptions of market analyses are often misleading. The self interest motivation of most economic analyses, the implied assumption of but minor interaction between the economic and political systems and the adjustive tendencies of both, and similar broad, general assumptions tend to blur or deny the significance of class, regional, non-economic interests i.e. political, moral and social differences and peculiarities.

An example often used in this regard is the concept of capital as applied to people – human capital, with the almost automatic tendency to apply to people the analytic techniques and terminology devised for things. Even if the non-differentiation between things and people is *analytically* effective, it tends to reduce the humanity of people with respect to politics, art, love, friendship and all the other attributes which people have but capital does not.

The refusal or inability of economics to deal with political, social, humane and other non economic resource considerations has led to two strange procedures. The *first* is for economists to define the problems so as to exclude as irrelevant such considerations which, in fact, are often exceedingly relevant in immediate economic situations as well as in their social acceptance. To deal with monetary policy and not to include unemployment or foreign policy (both of which go beyond economics) however would not be very effective. The *second* procedure is for the economist to homogenize the world being analyzed by assuming all the actors in the world have the same sort of "welfare function", that is they are all striving for the same hierarchy of utilities. If a group's or even person's behavior is explicable by some alien welfare function, some untoward effects on that person or group are assumed to be justified. If unemployed people won't leave N.Y. or anywhere else for Kokimo or Alaska where there are jobs, the blame is on them. Transfer costs, when considered, and who knows how to measure them, are often reduced to money alone.[2]

In general the ideal of economic analysis is to expose ways to maximize income. The economic system functions best when it is "efficient" for then it is legitimated. At the margin, a dollar of input yields a dollar of output.

Obviously efficiency requires a market with rules, inhibitions and constraints. These are all assumed away, in a sense, and various degrees of competition, freedom of entry and exit, divisibility of inputs, etc. are substituted as assumptions. Non competitive markets then are usually considered to be less efficient than competitive markets, although empirical analysis often finds to the contrary. Economies of scale and transfer costs are only slowly being integrated into micro analysis, while the amenity and welfare considerations, usually the results of legislation, are still generally considered as obstacles to efficiency.

Economics as a discipline seeks to be analytical. It is on analytical findings that business and economic policy and program are supposedly based. This necessarily implies some goal expectations.

Economic analysis is the extension of a set of relationships, actually perceived or believed implied (assumed), as being generally valid. That is to say some relationship, say between prices and costs in which price exceeds cost is conceptually posited. A causal explanation is then assumed based on the nature of the economic system which is posited. The insight might be that prices are higher than costs as a short run, transitory phenomenon related to supply of money or pent up demand, or some other cause. Then the observer analyst imagines how the difference will be adjusted, or if it will be adjusted, usually in some time span. A basic assumption here is the "tendency toward equilibrium".

Mathematical economics, using the symbolism of mathematics, manipulates these symbols in accordance with the rules of algebra, calculus, analytic geometry, and other mathematical techniques. Statistical economics uses perceived or estimated numbers and the manipulative techniques of statistics and mathematics. More traditional analysis relies on logic, factual data and mathematics, but largely on the logic of an equilibrial, closed system. All three factions of thought seem directed toward examining the nature, direction and intensity of changes toward equilibrium or stability, although in the past decade or so disequilibrial systems or circumstances have been sometimes introduced to the analysis.

In practice however, most economic analysis is *ad hoc*. Particular issues are isolated and analyzed as if they were not part of the greater whole. Neoclassical economics with its partial equilibrium approach is academically distinguishable from the total equilibrium approach. The British and American schools traditionally held to the former, more flexible way to look at the economy. The French and Italians followed the total approach. The total approach is more generally popular than it was 40 years ago. In analyzing a micro or macro problem economists of each school, depending on the insights and sophistication of the analyst, introduce considerations of politics, morality, personality and values.

The role of poiltical and social ideology then, is *implicit* in the analysis and advice provided. Analysis, to a degree, has predetermined the conclusions (and advice). Are monetarists, in the main, politically conservative because they are monetarists, or vice versa? Does Keynes appeal to liberals because of his method, or do liberals choose Keynes because of his goals? It is true that a Marxist can be a political conservative, but such a person would be a rare bird, indeed.

The natural sciences tend to reason from physical observations to attitudes and values about the phenomenon being observed. Social science often tends to do the reverse. To the physiologist molecules and medicine may affect the temper and temperament of the patient. To the psychologist the patient's temper and temperament may tend to affect the soma and its parts. Politicians think from social attitudes to numbers (of votes). Demographers think from numbers of people to population characteristics and behavior.

The designs of economic theory are generally not for problem solving.

They are designs to model a reality as perceived or hypothesized by economists (of a school). Yet the discipline is regularly directed toward problem solving.[3] Some economists acquire fame and fortune as stock market or other market, prognosticators. Their advice is often correct. From what we have argued such correctness is rarely inherent in the workings of a purely economic model. The observer – analyst has brought more to the job than the title "Economist" suggests.

Economists as a class of people often tend to oppose social reforms which redistribute income downward, or which transfer economic power to the less empowered classes and ideological groups. In truth, from my perspective, economists tend often to be correct – most reforms do not work as planned. But on the net, over the last 50 years or since the New Deal was born, the have nots and powerless group have improved their relative position, in accord, one may add, with democratic doctrine and social experiments. How much was due to economic reform or to market intervention, is hard to determine. But, on the net, a persuasive case can be made that many interventions of government into markets have been successful. The failures stand out.

Probably the law, even more than economics, envelopes and permeates all human activity connected with getting and spending. Criminal concerns, property matters, the family, inheritance, taxes, employee relations, all contracts, duties, rights and obligations, are major concerns of law. In brief the entire network of the connections between and among people, between and among people and social institutions, and between and among institutions are legally bound.

Like economic propositions and theories, legal propositions and theories are not generally agreed on. The traditional bases of law and its development, however are quite different from the bases of economic thought. Ideals of market efficiency and often argument and confusion regarding the economic effects of private and public amenity are among the main concerns of economics. Law on the other hand, in my view, is primarily concerned with holding the world together. That is modes of behavior are legitimated so the society can function without debilitating turmoil and dysfunction. Limits of acceptable behavior are determined and untoward deviations punished and corrected. Some kind of legitimated harmony is the ideal goal. The law is more complex than economics. Both have a public and private face, but economic behavior along with other private and social behavior *falls within the law*. Law encompasses economics and more. The adjustive aspects of law, the implications to be considered, include economic (market) activity as only one of its many social activities. Social efficiency, if that is an implied purpose of law, is not amenable to so simple an efficiency measure as costs and returns measured in money. Indeed the amenity aspects of markets e.g. ecological considerations, hours of work, validity of contracts, are usually introduced into the market via the law. That the law can act with only minor regard to the economic realities is a popular fallacy, leading to private and public disillusion and frustration. That economic decision making can ignore the law is to place the decision squarely at loggerheads with legitimation. By legitimation is meant the process by which an action is accorded public acceptance by a large fraction of the people.

The nature of law – including conventions, legislation, court and administrative rules, various decrees, and so on – is more complex than the nature of economic activity. The former is directed toward legitimizing behavior in general, the latter toward production and distribution of scarce goods and services. The former, the law, has no single conceptual market, the latter – economics – is resource and market bounded.

In spite of the cynical sophistication (of Justice Holmes) which asserts that law is not primarily concerned with justice, the law, as a legitimating social institution, inevitably is related to *some* conceptions of the right and good. If law only limits the bad, that is good. To be sure the right and the good are not identical for all people, at any time and place, or for all people over time and in different places. Right, wrong, good, bad are not situational in the sense that merely changing a superficial aspect of time and place, or some special or private attitude, automatically legitimates behavior. If, generally speaking, a society condemns price fixing, but a group of decent people trying to get an industry started, fix prices, the action *cannot* be legitimated on the grounds of situation. On the other hand stealing a loaf of bread to feed one's starving family does find a situational legitimation in the minds of many moralists. Most Americans and Europeans find the legal systems as well as specific laws of Hitler's Germany or Pinochet's Chile offensive. Judgment is always the ultimate recourse when the actions being evaluated are not congruent with preconceived ideas of appropriate behavior.

The courts are particular institutions to judge such behavior and judges do not rule strictly by precedent. One thrust of the realist legal doctrine is to suggest that judgments of courts, within limits, are in accord with the preconceptions of the judge.

It is to these limits we shall turn. Courts are the penultimate legal legitimators, short of the evanescent popular will. But courts have built in restraints to their legitimating capacity, restraints judges do not always recognize. In matters of science and morality e.g. how much benzene in the air is harmful; or in questions of military, political or social policy e.g. should the Japanese in W.W. II have been segregated in camps, or what constitutes price fixing which is harmful to consumers and competitors, the Courts are, generally speaking, simply not especially competent judges. All the Courts can do is assure that the legal and administrative processes which support the policy in question were observed. Judges, of course, sometimes do go beyond the set limits and make new law and policy, some good, some dubious.

As the knowledge of Courts in arcane non legal matters increases, due to the increase in general knowledge; as policy becomes less tentative, the certainty of the judges, too, will grow stronger. If, as in the school busing and segregation issues, legislatures and administrators are unwilling or unable to act with assurance, the Courts and the law do become the agencies to hold the world together. In the 1840s and later in the 1930s "judge made" law permitted unions legally to exist and grow. Without such innovation there was the possibility of social chaos. We refer, of course, to the Commonwealth vs. Hunt (Mass. 1848) and the string of labor – management decisions of the early F.D.R. days.

Legal doctrine, as we are using the concept, is the rationalization of how laws are made and administered. Law, in all societies, is a social agency for legitimating behavior. No matter how the laws or rules are made, for them to be effective there must be some social acceptance. Laws are generally obeyed and observed without constant recourse by government to violence and force. Without such legitimation there would be chaos.

Legitimation works both ways. Laws sanction behavior, and vice versa. In Hitler's Germany the laws were in fact generally observed, even though some groups and individuals objected and even refused to obey them. The greater social unacceptance was probably *outside* Germany, which ultimately led to the military defeat of the Nazi regime. But even before the Allies destroyed the Hitler Government, abortive internal attempts were made to exterminate Hitler and establish some more acceptable governance. At any rate the law of Hitler's Germany, by and large, was widely accepted, hence there was an overt or implied legitimation of social and political behavior within the Reich.

For the United States, and many other states of the world, the popular acceptance of the rules of governance are generally accepted, with little organized dissent. By far the great dissent in stable societies is to be found in the orderly, political opposition to the Government – the loyal, legal opposition. But both government supporters and the opposition, as well as non government groups, associations and individuals, tend to accept law as interpreted and administered by the courts, and other administrative bodies e.g. tax and criminal administration. To be sure criticisms are made, legislative reform bills introduced, public protests and approval are expressed privately and publicly. But the law, as evinced in the ruling in question, is generally accepted and is treated as legitimate even if wrong and dastardly.[4]

The legitimation of the law and public policy are tested to the extreme by revolution and threats of revolution. Short of revolutions there are crises in legitimation. In the 1960s and early 70s large fractions of the U.S. population were in virtual revolt, that is refused legitimation to many of the U.S. public policies. The war in Viet Nam was clearly a focus of attention denying legitimacy to the *status quo.* To many, in and out of politics, the idea of trying to impose a government and social system on an unlucky, impoverished people, half way around the world, seemed preposterous and immoral. To fight a war in Asia was apparent nonsense, to stop Communism in South East Asia a silly slogan, to conscript young men, primarily Blacks, outrageous, and so on. This major conflict against the policy *status quo* was supplemented by the Women's Movement (then Women's Lib) demanding equal economic and social rights with men, the youths' refusal to legitimate middle class standards with regard to sexual *mores,* drug use, criticisms of the morality of traditional economic markets, and of popular art forms in music and drawing. In short, new ways politically to announce an unwillingness to legitimate the *status quo* were flaunted. To further complicate the already muddy scene, the middle class, middle aged, in various ways, including language, dress, sexual mores and political nihilism, supported, wittingly or unwittingly, revolting youth.

3 The Legitimation Process

The counterforces of the old time religion, the Moral Majority, the new political conservatism and social "laid backness", of course, appeared. They became politically successful in the elections of Carter and later Reagan.

Young, successful people, that is those who had made it by the age of 40 or less, were the heirs of the mid century turbulence. By and large those in the middle and high income groups accept the idea of social concern. "The poor and the disadvantaged, the old and the infirm should be the concern of the government. Nuclear war is a real threat, and nuclear defense a necessity. But–taxes are too high (too high for what is rarely explained). Government tends to be too intrusive. (Get government off our backs). Income taxes should be at a flat rate–that is only fair. Such taxes are also easy to compute. Sure–social concerns are desirable and even necessary, but I think I'll vote my pocketbook." This was the yuppie ideology. The election of '84 and '88 pretty clearly exposed the schizoid nature of the political, hence moral, personality of large groups in the United States.

The reaction to social movements and the social movements themselves do not happen with only a moment's notice. Social and political alignments slowly emerge. A new ideology is engendered. The old leadership is cast aside and a new one fashioned. The ponderous process provides the time and legitimation for an opposing movement. The composition of the new social and political movement, is not monolithic, but usually made up of interest groups which move in and out of the alliances.

At one time the Women's Movement and the Black Movement made common cause, now they are quite separate. At one time the South was solidly Democratic. In 1980 all Southern states except Georgia voted for Reagan, and Bush was strong in the South in 88. It would not be surprising if in the next decade the Women's Movement became more politically conservative while the Trade Union movement more radically demanding of the political system. Polarity in social life is not like the polarity of a magnet. The constituent parts of the society shift their positions and attitudes and change their ideologies, hence legitimations. Ideologies are but values in action, and new times and circumstances change both the values and the actions.

Why such changes and variance in attitude are usually not revolutionary is related to the ideologic content and verbalized legitimation of what is sought. A revolutionary movement looks for change with the explicit caveat that a *new* administrative system, power structure and special goals are needed and wanted. The old authorities, the old way of doing the world's work simply are no longer relevant. The frequency of American election, every 2, 4 and 6 years tends to deter the revolutionary approach to change.

Such a view was, so far as we can fathom, part of the upheaval of the 60s and 70s. True enough a few people, often young people chalked the slogan "all power to the people" on walls and bridges. This was, in our view, vulgar sloganeering. A deep structural change was not envisaged. Individual leaders had to go, and President Johnson did go. Particular authorities as the police, the courts, and the universities were criticized for *not* doing their jobs properly. But their *functions* were not attacked. *In brief the social thrust was to return to the ideals of society which had been lost by being abused or frittered away.* The Communist Party USA, and other radical organizations, came out of the maelstrom no stronger and probably weaker than they entered it. Motorcycle gangs, in the U.S., are more terroristic than leftwing political groups. The past 1960–70 era seems one more devoted to reform of the society and its politics than to destroying them.

The New Deal was probably more consciously orchestrated and controlled than the psychotic '60s and '70s. The New Deal leadership viewed itself as the shield *against* revolution, as the safeguard of the *status quo as it should be*. The weakness of the New Deal was lack of technical expertise, if, in fact, such expertise existed. The weakness was not romanticism. The '60s and '70s, in spite of the slogans, was a *status quo ante* movement, a romanticism.

Laws and administrative rules obviously change with changes in legislation and also with social changes. Courts, administrative bodies, legislation all operate in a social milieu, and are part of the format. However, the sensitivity to change, the speed of reaction, the mortmain of the past, the persistence of ideologies, class, professional and more generally social, tend to make change very uneven.

The law and its administration, that is today's public administrators and courts, and the legislature, if they are to do their duty of "holding the world together," must take into account the realities of the situation, now and in the future. Yet each is constrained by his or her own ideology, experience, and morality as well as by the built in institutional constraints. Judges tend to act like judges, administrators like administrators. Ms. Anne Burford, formerly head of the Environmental Protection Administration, resigned under fire, and later was appointed to chair an ecological advisory board. Both houses of Congress passed resolutions deploring her appointment. Ms. Burford, however went further and denigrated the political actions and reactions by publicly declaring the new post to be a "nothingburger." In effect she attacked the institution to which she was appointed and, by inference, the President who appointed her, as well as the ecological issues she was to deal with. The result is she was forced to withdraw or did so voluntarily upon reflection of the social and political crime she had committed. She did not act like a public administrator and probably will not again have that opportunity.

4 The Rates of Change

The consideration of the manner, purpose and background of court decisions, administrative rulings and political behavior have attracted the interest of legal and social scholars. Is the law the reflection of some natural, absolute, or perhaps transcendental, or Platonic manifestation. And are reasoning people bound to obey such law? After all Platonic idealism is at the base of some current physical theory, why not apply it to legal theory, which is nearer its historic origin than its application to physics? Or is the law constrained by a long chain of precedents which may be cut and fit to time and circumstance; but essentially are the basis of legal continuity? This view may be refashioned to hold that legal decisions tend to reflect the interests of the decision maker or his class. The two general views, the absolute and the self or class interest are presented boldy as antitheses.

Conservatism vs. Realism, or Creative Traditionalism vs. Sensitive Legitimation are the two rationalizing forces. Each in my opinion has some persuasive qualities, but neither is entirely nor persistently correct as a mode of explanation.

Conservatism or Creative Traditionalism (CT) tends to stress *stare decisis,* or precedent principles of equity and morality which are persistent and invariant rules of conduct, which are to be expected in any social circumstance. On the other hand Realism or Sensitive Legitimation (SL) tends to stress, as explanatory reasons for the rules of behavior and law, the interests and values of judges, administrators, and the parties involved. The rules are tempered by what is happening socially and the changes related to what is happening. Traditional rules are, in effect, adjusted to the reality of the time. In such reality are not only economic interests of the involved parties, but the social and historic interests of government, courts and the social welfare, as interpreted by judges. Even after political revolutions designed to "change the system" the realities of the past persist. Is the Soviet Union a different world in essence from Czarist Russia? Were the American Colonies a different society after the Revolution?

The two extremes of persistence and tentative change, of traditionalism and realism are not at loggerheads. In point of experience Conservatism or Creative Traditionalism recognized that women are in the labor market to stay, that black families need garbage collection and paved streets, and that the abortion issue is still unresolved. In short the C/CT explanation accepts the idea that the world and its values are changing, and the law and Courts must keep pace or lose their legitimacy. The Realism/Sensitive Legitimation is cast in a similar mold, but the speed and degree of reaction are greater than in the C/CT view. R/SL stresses the word sensitive. C/CT may react more slowly than R/SL but that is rationalized as being careful. Perhaps to C/CT one should add careful.

The courts and law seem to change in waves or spurts. It is as if a dam of tradition and precedent hold back change until the pressure becomes so great that the dam is burst. The post Civil War period, the turn of the century, the New Deal, the 1960s and 70s represent such periods of reorientation. The content of civil and criminal laws, the application and interpretation of law, the expectations of the majority and minorities, the national self image all change, say, over a decade, to be moderately quiescent for another decade or so.

Economic and business theorizing change in much the temporal fashion as the law's theorizing. It is often at the end of an economic era that the social and managerial theories of the era are devised, developed and dethroned. But the ideas and ideals carry on into the next period. The changes in economic and legal thinking come not in one fell swoop, not sharply and definitively. The changes are often imperceptible, backing and filling in the short term, but moving ineluctably forward to a new vague ending which is never reached.

That economic reality affects both economic theory and the law, and hence legal theory, cannot be denied. To the extent that the totality of modern society is so consciously oriented toward getting and spending, to that extent the law has to be economically oriented. That the legal argument in the past 50 years has accepted more and more economic logic and argument, is I believe, apparent. The opposite however is less true. Economics, as a discipline, has not appreciably incorporated legal precepts to any large degree. Nor has the nature of law struck out into the new and less traditional economic theorizing. Yet both kinds of cross fertilization are needed as a synthesis to keep our social rules relevant. And it will occur. How well and with what social sensitivity and sophistication is the question. And it is a question which the Schools and Universities should face, but, up to now have been reluctant dragons.

5 Criticism and Legitimation

We have asserted that economics, – getting and spending – is a more restricted concern than the law. We have asserted this because the law engulfs and legitimates all aspects of economics, constraining and restraining the business exercise. The reverse is not always true. Even the Marxian social engine which is dominated by technology, resources and self interest, requires social legitimation to supplant self interest by some pan-social dedication. To supplant self interest by some general social interest requires legitimation. If the bourgeois law cannot or will not do the job, a new legitmation has to be developed, *viz* the legitimation of socialism, indeed international socialism. Finally international socialism is supposed to legtimate Utopia which will then become ideology!

This scenario is not acting itself out very well. A non utopian, but real value system has become the legitimating power, in short the law in the various national communist states. So the law in current Marxist eastern states as well as in the moderate socialist and other western societies continues to justify the economic and market systems and adjust them (more or less) in accord with the requirements of due process. Law holds the world together even though both the world and the law are themselves incomplete, often shoddy, and not at all of a seamless extension.

I am not an expert in the theory or theories of the law. Try as hard as I will to free myself, I find the limited logic, the defined universe, the ruliness of economics part of my automatic thinking. This habit persists in spite of the fact that the economic realities are often not even roughly congruent with economic theory. In a sense, to be an effective theorist one must "impound" great hunks of reality in *ceteris paribus* and *pari passu*. That other things are not equal, and that the hinterland of the universe of discourse does not automatically adjust, are realities that tend to frustrate equilibrial solutions, or at least workable solutions, to many economic problems. Time is not a homogenous flow in all the parts and functions of the real world, nor do long run problems permit of simultaneous solutions.

Yet if one wants to try to make some sense of the exciting, fluctuating real world with its exogenously as well as endogenously caused movements, then staid, economic theory, abstracting from the maelstrom of reality all that can be abstracted and still have a structure, is the only tool I know for generalized, abstract analysis. The finer, the coarser, the mystical and transcendental, the just, the fair and good elements of social life are impounded, along with certain forces, when the observer feels them to be of minor significance, of the second order of small as my cerebral student colleagues at the University of Chicago would say, long ago.

The law as a legitimating factor is among the impounded. Private ownership, the market, individual and collective rights are all there, but unchanging and inactive as causative forces. Their essences, their spirits, along with the essences of many economic quantities are for the time being "held constant". Of course the first exercise is supposed to be a first approximation. Second, third, and so on to "n" analytic steps are to be taken so that the analytic universe finally includes the impounded forces. The sad truth, however, is that only rarely, if ever, are the second, third and "n" approximation to reality ever made. Nor would the ordinarily trained economist know what further approximations to make.

An engineering colleague with whom I discussed this approach to knowledge over dinner, vigorously objected. He argued a Geiger Counter works. That's all there is to it. The proof of the pudding is in the eating and not in philosophy, metaphysics or ontology. He refused to agree that although one may accept the Geiger Counter as effective, there may be alternative ways to explain why and how the counter works.

The charm and value of economics are that it attempts to put together the *framework* of an economic system. Some ideologues would assert it is the only or the best framework to explain reality. But, as we have argued, reality is a species of fantasy at most, or assumption at best. It only makes sense if a number of communicants agree generally on the assumptional set and on the nature of the generating forces e.g. self interest and technology. Then the communicants can, in truth and fact, communicate with each other intelligibly. Then changes can be made in the structural framework and its adjustments.

The law, as it is, and has been made and applied, is more down to earth, more directly effective than the application of economics. The economist as legislator, manager, and analyst, is, or should be, exactly as impure and realistic, as adaptive as the lawyer, manager, analyst, judge and legislator. "How will it play in Peoria?" is a vague but appropriate question. Can it- the decision-be lived with or will it gum up the works, does it have equity and justice? Is it ethical? These are all considerations which cannot be denied.

Judgment is the *ultimate* vehicle of legitimation. And judges are, generally speaking, the ultimate formal judgment makers. The final makers of the social judgments of course are the people of the society. They may, in their time, which never seems to move fast enough, undo the judges and laws, change *stare decisis,* recast insitutions. While waiting for such grand changes to take place, the reliance is formally pleaded on judges, among whom we include public administrators applying the law and the rules.[5]

Judges, like pure economists, impound knowledge, often never to let it out of the pound. But the impounding is not so formal and possibly so automatic in law as in economics. In economics whatever is deemed irrelevant, is impounded in *ceteris paribus* or *pari passu,* for the moment, often never to be heard from again. In the law the judge asks himself of what must he or she take judicial notice. And there are pleading lawyers to sway his notice.

There are styles in judicial behavior. Some jurists are wider in their perceptions of what affects or goes into decision making than other. Some jurists lean more to precedent, others toward the social setting of the issues to be decided. Legislative intent, constitutional interpretation, narrow or broad construction of statute and precedent, are all elements in the judicial input to a decision. And the inputs, values and logics of different judges lead them to differ in their findings. One has the impression that some judges are more politically conservative than others. The decisions of courts, the reversal of lower courts, the tone and nature of opinions and *obiter dicta,* clearly tell us that judges are neither clones of each other nor in agreement as to their perceptions of and their expectations for the world.

A tiny example, shallow in its implications, illustrates the variety of interests and judgments. Chief Justice Burger, speaking before the American Bar Association in August 1983 was reported as castigating lawyers for the vulgar advertisements of their services in the press on radio and television. He likened the advocational pitches to the ''come on'' ads for hair tonic and dog food. He gave the lawyers hell, in short, for not acting with the dignity of lawyers, as he perceived that dignity.

The same day Mr. Justice Stevens, dedicating a new building at a University, berated his Brothers of the Bench for unecessarily going out of their way to agree to hear and decide cases which did *not* need hearing and adjudication. The Supreme Court, he held, was in error for trying to improve of policy of the nation by its conceptions, and extending Congressional policy beyond what statute required. It was at once an attack on the conservative wing of the court for pushing conservatism beyond the Congressional intent and also for filling in gaps in the law with conservative plaster.

Economists, too, vary in their social ideas of what is good policy, and in their ideas of what is relevant for useful analysis. The 1983 Nobel Laureat in economics was Professor Gerard Debreu[6] the French born American theorist. He told us, in his acceptance lecture, of the extraordinary privilege of working with other famous colleagues in extending the theory of general equilibrium to make it more rigorous and extensive; and for solving problems in theories preference, utility and demand. The analytical techniques were (often) "borrowed from diverse fields of mathematics".[6] One may suggest that the more refined the assumptions the less useful the conclusions are in their direct application of the social problems. This is not an adverse criticism. Research may or may not be directly useful as a public device. Usefulness here is not the purpose. Knowledge, insight and just plain enjoyment are their own excuses for being. Our point is that all of economics is not designed to solve work-a-day problems.

At another extreme is Nobel Laureate – Herbert Simon. Simon has long been interested in social behavior generally. What Simon seems to be after, in his theoretical work, is an explanation of actual behavior. He finds that traditional economics theory does "not always lead to the same conclusions at the level of aggregate phenomena and policy as are implied by the postulate of bounded rationality, in any of its variants".[7] The limited, testable generalization is to be preferred to the grand generalizations of pure, unbounded rational theory.

Yet Stevens and Burger, Simon and Debreau have much in common. That the law as an institution requires obedience in a well ordered society, that the law reflects some idea of justice (although there is disagreement as to what justice is or should be), that the Supreme Court is the ultimate court of the land, and so on, are generally accepted views. Such views tend to be formal and structural rather than views of particular substance. People disagree with courts and law in respect to social content and also, to an extent, in what is appropriate behavior. Economists tend to agree on the subject matter they are concerned with – resources, preferences, income, etc. They disagree, it seems to me, most in their methodological and epistemological perceptions. Debreu stands firmly on the platform of mathematics with its logical supports, ignoring as any active researcher is likely to, the realistic application of the logical assumptions. But to do so is to ask Debreau to spend his time guessing on what Atlas, who carries the World on his shoulders, stands. Or in spending his time explaining the extension of space. Debreau accepts that he is, can think, that he can communicate. Simon accepts the ongoingness of the world, but in segments. He tries to understand and explain the parts that interest him, not the whole of it all at once. And being proud and serious, he gives his theoretical opponents what for.

Stevens and Burger – Debreu and Simon – are not the extremes of their disciplines. They are people who help us understand, in this exercise, that the limits of law and economics are not fixed and merely factual; that the two disciplines are not neat, orderly, regular geometric planes or spaces. Law and economics, and other social disciplines, wander, expand, shrink, change their subject matter, indeed reflect the minds, efforts, findings, and behavior of people who are called, or call themselves lawyers, judges, or economists.

That Simon's work is more relevant to my interests makes him neither a better economist nor a better, more correct man and observer than Debreau. They are following different paths in the same universe of discourse, broadly defined. Nor is Stevens a better or worse judge than Burger because one has an interest in judicial and legislative authority, the other in appropriate behavior of lawyers. In deciding an issue Simon and Debreau, or Burger or Stevens can be compared, and of course evaluated, by the criteria of the earth bound evaluator and not only by a Higher Standard known only to God.

Nevertheless what the Justices represent *is* a higher standard (with no capitals) than what Debreu and Simon represent, insofar as the first pair represent the *ultimate* legal legitimation. The latter provide only a market legitimation. That the law can be changed by the legislature or by judges keeps the capital letters from ever being attached to the higher standard. The Court is the earthly ultimate – the last recourse of formal legitimation, as things stand. Things are not always constant. Legal legitimation can change as can economic. Absolutes in theory or practice should have no place in our thoughts, politics or expectations.

It is persuasion which finally carries the day in such a welter of misunderstanding. And persuasion is a face of compromise. What am I persuaded to support, and at what cost, and with what benefits, including in those social considerations of appropriate behavior, are the stuff of getting agreement.

Compromise and responsibility are the *sine quo non* of the American society and Western society generally. The great market compromises of our society are over individualism and amenity. Such compromises expressed as law or policy are not fixed for all time.

In short we suggest that the compromise between individual rights and private and public amenities is a major element in law and its administration. And compromises are sometime things. They become unstuck under the pressures and forces of new issues and new circumstances, they become obsolete and hindrances to behavior, and are abolished, and replaced. This does *not* mean that right and wrong are legitimated with absolute differences in different times and places. For the Soviet Union to jail or "hospitalize" a person because he or she is critical of the regime is improper. This view is not based on Soviet law, nor on some higher law, but rather on the moral precepts and perceptions of justice of the generality of western societies. We have *our* standards, and judge by them. This is moral imperialism of a sort. So what? Even granting Western values are *not* absolute does not afford any moral or other legitimating cloak to the

Soviet rules. The same applies to other behavior modes of other societies including our own.

Realism and reasonable compromise are not the solutions to all problems, but they do solve many. Judgment is the way to legitimacy, and legitimacy is implicit in a reasonable compromise. Judgment and compromise are contained in the law emergent.

Footnotes

[1] K. E. Boulding – *The Organizational Revolution,* Especially the Preface-Quadrangle 1968.
[2] J. M. Keynes "The General Theory of Employment," Quarterly J. of Economics p. 212–223, 1937.
[3] cf. J. R. Hicks *Capital and Growth* – Oxford 1965 for a magnificant essay which lacks a useful setting.
[4] P. A. Freund *On Law and Justice,* Belknap-Harvard 1968 – Ch. 1, "The Court and the Constitution. This is a fairly conservative view.
[5] G. W. Paton *Jurispondence* – Oxford 1946 See Ch. 1 "The Nature of Jurispondence" for a summary of legal theories.
[6] G. Debreu – "Economic Theory in the Mathematical Mode," *Am. Ec. Rev.,* June '84.
[7] H. A. Simon, "Rational Decision Making in Business Organizations" *Am. Ec. Rev.,* September '79.

Chapter VIII
Professionalism and Business Ethics

1 Profession as an Idea

What does society want of those who serve it? Largely services which satisfy the wants asked of those who purport to do so. The wants are often more than those bargained overtly for. Politeness, friendliness, an attractive milieu, and other amenities are expected. When the service required is run of the mill, the ambience becomes important in dividing suppliers into classes, price classes for example. A great compliment to a supplier of services is to assert the services are "professional". Profession and professional, however, are not the same.

Is business a profession? Not stated another way, but really a different question is: Are business people professionals? It is with this question that we shall begin.

A professional, we hold as a useful definition, is one who, as a usual matter, performs some action for hire or for personal recompence. The oldest professional occuption in the world often is supported by a professional manager. Neither person is engaged in a profession, or as the older phrase had it a "learned profession". My roof is repaired by a professional roofer after I refused the services of my son-in-law who is both a professional scientist and a member of a scientific profession. What lies back of the distinctions I am making?

A professional is anyone who earns his or her living performing certain defined tasks, although one has heard of a professional general handyman. Most tasks require some training, and the several levels of training are of different durations and degrees of difficulty. The hairdresser is a professional but in current (or at least in our) language is not a member of a profession. The lawyer on the other hand is in a profession by most classi-

143

fications (sometimes lawyers do not behave professionally). Yet both lawyer and hairdresser take courses of study and have to pass some governmentally approved examinations to get a license. The license permits one to work in a field, and by itself involves no status of profession.

The three years of law school, the presumably searching nature of the law examinations, including the consideration of the applicant's moral stature and value system are involved in making the law a profession or learned profession. Both professionals, attorney and hairdresser, are subjected to approval by peer or governmentally imposed ethical standards. But the significance, in a societal sense, of the lawyer's ethical requirements are supposedly "loftier" and more "demanding" than those of the hairdresser.

Whether, in fact, hairdressers are more or less *ethical* than lawyers is, of course, an open question. That the ethical constraints and restraints of lawyers should be higher is, I presume, an accepted idea, so long as one does not try to spell out the ethical canons of either calling. Professional, in common parlance is any one who performs a task with neatness and dispatch. Grass can be cut, or a battle fought, or a house built in "a professional fashion".

Business people, by whom I mean managers, that is people who have a responsibility for the operation of a firm or part of a firm, with the authority to make decisions of some moment on their own, are not licensed nor subjected to any *required* course of study. They are professionals insofar as they are employed as managers and make a living thereby. But are they members of a profession? Is there a peer pressure or accepted behavior constrained from within a peer group, apart from legal or market requirements? Is there a unique code of ethics formally promulgated or informally imposed by peers on the person in question? In general the answer is in the negative, but in specific circumstances the answer is in the affirmative but often with a question mark. Peer pressure on a free wheeling manager may be interpreted as a conspiracy as in a price fixing caper.

There are no *public* examinations which qualify one as an economist or statistician. There are examinations certifying public accountants, insurance experts or engineers. Are the latter three members of various professions or merely members of some associations or classified occupations? They are often responsible to, and take orders from, a business person (manager) who possibly lacks formal education and any state certificate.

The certified expert, member of some association and/or licensed, is always subject to peer pressure. He or she will be possibly read out of the association or lose his/her license, if the written or merely understood canons of professional propriety are violated, even if the boss directs such improper conduct. But is the boss, either directly or indirectly, the object of the peer pressure in ethics or professional conduct, of the association or agency which certified the employee members of the profession? Not exactly is the appropriate answer. Too much peer pressure can invite a conspiracy suit.

2 Business as a Calling, not as a Profession

The professional manager is not a member of a managerial-entrepreneurial profession because there is no such body. Perhaps the manager is so general in his/her responsibility and skill that no peer pressure is possible. But the professional manager is not exempt from *social* pressure. If he or she earns or is accorded a poor reputation as a manager, or as an honest, honorable person, the market pressures operate to produce a result similar to that of peer pressure – to wit the manager loses or gains status. He/she is passed up for jobs or promotions, or wins them. Salary at customary levels is denied or granted, the person is shunned or accepted. And there is no recourse open to the manager. At a more prosaic level of behavior members of a profession often may be insured against technical misadventures. Managers cannot be so protected.

Companies and trade associations, sometimes promulgate canons of ethics as self determined constraints and restraints. As significant as these may be, and some represent lofty sentiments, they do not create a profession. They merely define professionalism for their members.

Profession implies a status which may be formally or informally bestowed. The status symbol does not shine equally for the different professions – the landscape architect is not usually accorded the same respect the more prestigous architect who builds skyscrapers; or the country horse doctor is not accorded the same status the Harvard Professor of Neurosurgery. Similarly the Harvard Professor is deemed to be entitled to greater respect than the rural family M.D. Assuming economics to be a profession, the new Ph.D. from the U. of Arizona is not usually accorded the status shown the ancient professor of economics at the U. of Chicago. So the social and business status of the successful big business magnate is generally superior to the status of the successful owner-manager of the Amherst Laundromat.

145

Status seems bifurcated. It is related to power and success as well as to a hierarchy of activities (professions as well as merely professional occupations).

All in all then, business management, regardless of the status of any individual, seems not includable in the ranking of professions. From the viewpoint of the market, business ethics is not unimportant for it is considered in the ranking of a person who is being judged as a professional or in a profession. Decency is measured not by license or state examination nor by college degrees or titles. The ethical decency of a person is in the judgement of the people who observe and have opinions about the person in question.

One of the active functions of a profession is to mark out a class of peers who are, in effect, the guardians of the technical requirements of the profession as well as of its ethics. Ethics is part of the rules of behavior. Since management, as we hold, does not rely only on scientific revelation, and so is not organizable into a set of rules of technical behavior, the business person cannot be judged by adherence to or departure from approved techniques. There is no "state of the art" for the manager. Furthermore peer pressure is singularly absent, and is replaced by market pressure.

Business schools and schools of management, dedicated to the ideal of scientific management, may expose rules and scientific principles, but these are not, and in a free economic society cannot ever be, the only tools at the disposal of managers. Free will, chance, intelligence and imagination are uncurbed to operate in particular cases. The interesting and perhaps important parts of business are the particular cases.

It is the discontinuity of the current decision with those of the past which distinguishes the managerial decision maker from the mere administrator. The insights into the nature of the situation, the grasp of the potential of the available resources, the willingness to risk, the concern with success often seem to swamp the ethical implications of the managerial act. If this is so the manager is neither a complete person nor the perfect manager. He/she is always in the act of becoming, and never in the status of being. Becoming, hence a need for concern with ethics, is found in any and all social actions. The moral content may be large or small, but it is there as a residual of the social ideologies which encompass all social behavior. The ethic of the manager, hence of business, is part of the social ethic, not merely of the professional ethic or the ethic of a profession.

3 From Ethic to Rule

The ethics or moral stance of a limited segment of society–of a profession–is not the same as the ethics of a whole society, or of any particular activity. The social ethic, whatever it is taken to mean, is not the sum of the smaller ethics including private ethics. All are related but not in any additive way.

A private ethic we define as the moral values held by a person. To be sure he/she is the product of society and its value, but the merest experience illustrates that on many issues and in many behaviors there are nuances and marked differences in perceptions of right and wrong. On a larger scale members of a class are often bound by the class imposed values. Tradition, history and ideology lead carpenters who are recognized craftsmen to behave in certain ways both technically and morally. The looser the group the looser the constraints. It is not unknown for a tradesman to do shoddy work with shoddy materials. The client is likely to be stuck with the bad job. It is less likely for a surgeon knowingly to supply shoddy materials or consciously do sloppy work. The organization, formal and informal, of surgeons is closer and tighter than that of carpenters. Lawyers, physicians and probably engineers have or are supposed to have an intrusive peer group oversight which carpenters or stenographers do not have.

It is not merely competition, the market forces of acceptance or non acceptance, which lead to success or failure of those in closely monitored groups, it is also the group's acceptance or rejection. This idea is not at all new, but it is strangely absent in much of economic or market analysis. Incompetent members of a profession may lose their accreditation.

Self interest is assumed to be not only a motive force or prime mover in economic affairs, it is also assumed to be, within the limits of law, free to choose the means to gain the ends sought. If one assumes that businesses are controlled by owner-managers in a competitive setting, the power of self interest and the even spread of knowledge may be a useful set of assumptions. But if one assumes that large corporations are the suppliers of services, and they operate in large markets with great complexities of means, ends and imposed constraints, as is generally the case, the idea of self interest and knowledge as being somehow intuitively grasped by managers is not directly applicable. There are, we assert, corporate cultures which encompass not only matters of organization and structure, but also matters of appropriate behavior (morality) and goals.

Minorities and women, for example, until recent years rarely moved above some fairly well, predetermined level of authority in business generally or even in some professions. Such denial, in retrospect, gives rise to a moral evaluation. At the time of the restriction, morality was rarely involved. After the issue gains legal and public recognition, the moral aspects grow large. However as the legal and public attitude gain in strength and become widespread the moral issue is often, not so much replaced as superceded by the legal issue. In short suits are brought against offending parties who deny women's rights because equality of job opportunity has become a legal and not merely a moral right.

Within the firm the several divisions and parts are guided by subordinate, technical personnel, who are subordinate to the manager. The technical personnel may be engineers, accountants, lawyers or financial experts. The first three of the four examples are clearly members of professional groups in addition to being employees. The fourth, the financial expert, is a member of an organized group which has not as yet become so recognized a profession as the other three. The rules of the professions or emerging professions are, in effect, constraints and restraints on the actions of the members. Their self interest has been directed so it cannot automatically accept the direction of the manager on all scores. The lawyer who offers legal opinions merely to please his client is in trouble. The accountant who "cooks the books" is not likely to remain an accountant for long. There is an inner network of restraint and constraint within the large firm which is independent of the perceived managerial self interest. When, as, and if this network of morality (and also of knowledge) in interfered with by management, the adverse repercussions for all concerned may be serious. The Ivan Boesky case of insider trading in the U.S. is in point.

The moral aspects of the firm, then, are analogous to the moral aspects – the social ethic – of a society. Such aspects are often self contradictory and give rise to inefficiencies in the eyes of those who embrace and are embraced by other moral values.

The large firm then relies on moral, and technological resources, which are quite different from those of the owner-manager. This applies even if the owner manager has control over great resources but does not rely on subordinates with their own roots in their own professions.

This discussion tends to cast doubt on applying the self interest paradigm to corporations or markets unless it is modified to account for the necessary limitations and redirections implied by organization, structure, resources and built in moral restraints. Such built in moral restraints come not only from the origanizations of the professions and professionals, but also from government. Such forces may be viewed as various kinds of social ethics being social pressures. They are, we hold, different in nature and social function from the personal ethics which induce (or restrain) an individual toward (or from) certain actions. The social ethics, on grand or minor scale, are built *into* the social structure which tends to impose uniform individual behavior of the persons directly involved.

Chapter IX
The Jurisprudence of Markets and Business

1 The Setting

Regulatory legislation has pitfalls and difficulties. The logic of regulation is almost always at the mercy of the setting in which the regulation occurs. The social ethic is not accomplished by passing a law. Every phenomenon short of the entire universe has a setting. A society, a tree, an idea or a person does not exist in the total vacuum of space. Meaning, significance, use, and nature of something are part of the environment in which it is found just as are physical environments. Environment, according to dictionary meaning is the aggregate of *surrounding* things and influences affecting the existence and development of something. To this external view of environment we should add an internal view of, let us make up a word, *invironment*. By invironment we mean the aggregate of internal things and influences which affect the existence, meaning, and development of the phenomenon being considered. Trees have bark, sap, leaves, molecules, and so on endlessly which, when interacting make the tree. The tree is also a raw material for the lumber industry as well as an integral part of a forest. A person has character, a liver, hair, a mind, a brain, and so on, which make up the person. A person is also part of a group.

What we are saying is that there seems to be a necessary set of relationships between environmental and invironmental considerations. Let us then combine the two ideas in the single commonly used word "environment". Business environment then, for our discussion means the forces and structures, or influences and things, which affect markets and business. Internal organization of the firm and of the market are as implicit in the business and market environment as the ecological considerations of water, air, or noise, or public policies with respect to trade unions, ecology, taxes, price level or truth in advertising.

At the one extreme of environment there are the non-material ideas. At the other extreme are the physical, scientific and technological realities. Are there new material sources? Does sufficient knowledge exist to accomplish what is intended? Is capital available? Skill? Organizational ability? In between are issues of equity, attitudes toward kinds of energy investments, employment, safety, insurance and a list of other considerations and potential problems.

Ideology – values in action as a societal category – is a catch all which doesn't quite catch all. People as individuals have ideas about values which are not necessarily part of a socially crystallized set of values or behavior habits. For example, after World War II and for twenty years there was a fairly strong view among public utility managers and investors that nuclear power was to be a major energy source of the future. Politicians agreed. There was a concerted push toward nuclear power based on the belief it was the effective and efficient solution to the energy problems of the U.S. Technological and business investments appeared so satisfactory to persons with power to influence investments and market structures that the point of view attained a value status. It was the "right" thing to do from a business and social point of view. Right, as a correct course of action, because it was a legitimated, hence a social, moral, course of action.[2]

Yet some held out against this point of view. Early in the process of socially legitimating nuclear power, objectors were seen as die hards who were holding on to the dead past of thermal and water power. But later, as time progressed and as more knowledge about the dangers, cost and uncertainties connected with nuclear power were exposed, the opposition to the new energy source was itself legitimated into an ideology.

The process of modifying the investment perceptions of most die hards took some time because of the enormous appeal of nuclear power toward a more reasonable, critical attitude. The new opposition consisted of individuals whose contra position was not at first particularly accepted by any appreciable group of investors and experts. It is certainly not a group opposition with very much social power. The new opposition, however, stressed the dangers implicit in nuclear power production as well as the high costs of production. Strangely the risk element has not been connected to the high costs of insurance which the dangers of nuclear power production *should have entailed* which full insurance coverage required. Instead, the safety argument was (1) there never has been a melt down, and (2) the engineers know what they are doing. Just as the Great Depression, in a sense, pierced the balloon of the credibility of the economics profession, so Three Mile Island and the Challenger debacle (not a nuclear device) pierced the balloon of engineering credibility. Chernobyl, in the Soviet Union strengthened the anti-nuclear opposition, Engineers, like Keynsian economists, have been sent to the back of the room by critics who, it may be allowed, are on the whole unlearned in the arts they are criticizing.

The attitudes of business in the matter of nuclear power and its use became polarized over time. Legitimated views, business and political, both support and are dubious of great reliance, being placed on nuclear energy sources. Both positions have developed technological, political, economic, hence socially legitimated (ideological) arguments defending or attacking an extended reliance on nuclear energy. One crystallization of attitude about nuclear energy is around the high construction costs of facilities. Virtually no nuclear plant comes in at the estimated cost. Cost overruns and technical problems are the rule not the exception. The other attitude crystallization is about the environmental threat of nuclear power. One part of the opposition questions the economics of nuclear power, the other part the social consequences.

The pro side seems to hold that there are no long run feasible alternatives because new hydro power sites and carbon fuels are growing very scarce. Wind, solar, and natural energy resources have not as yet been developed. Nuclear is all we have for the ensuing period to rely on.

This gives us a first conceptual breakdown for any discussion of business environment. Whether discussing nuclear energy, the public budget or ecology, the relevant issues can be logically separated into (a) those which affect and influence a market and social decisions from the outside; and (b) those which affect social and market decisions from within. But this distinction may be misleading. Any *outside environmental* force or factor is only effective to the degree it changes or affects *internal structure and behavior*. This observation contains a can of philosophical worms. It is customary, and indeed at least for a century and a half usual, to consider the forces of history, e.g., technology and ideology, as controlling the flow of great events. Individuals concerned played roles which were and are essentially minor. But by our analysis the great social and historical forces are only felt when, as, and if they change the thinking and behavior of individuals who are both leaders and followers. How this synthesis of the environmental and invironmental forces takes place in social situations is a major problem of the social disciplines. In economics the so called micro–macro synthesis or the Neo classical – Keynsian synthesis has not been successfully explained. Nor have micro-macro interplays and defendencies been explained in many other disciplines. A forest is more than a collection of trees and a group of people is not meaningfully analyzed by generalizing from observations of individual behavior. Yet the world acts *as if* such syntheses occur under our noses. Individuals deeply believe what the social forces require to become effective. Or at least sometimes believe so. How many great historical tides were never realized because people did not react we'll never know.[3]

In brief the external environment by itself is neutral. It becomes effective in the process and as a result of being internalized by some group, activity, institution or person. Hence external *environment's* significance is in its *invironmental* processes.

The study and evaluation of the internalization process is, in part, the task of the micro disciplines of the social sciences and management. The process of internalization of environmental matters in business and social institutions ultimately deals with such internal matters as self interest, motivation, organization, structure, resource allocation, etc. Economics, accounting, sociology, marketing, anthropology, social and individual psychology are among the social analysis disciplines relied on. What is intriguing in the example we have drawn on, namely in the legitimation of nuclear energy, no one seems to have guessed or estimated beforehand, and expressed with sufficient persuasiveness the drawbacks. Costs of construction would be high. Safety would be a costly item and hard to attain. Ways of disposal would be a social and technical nightmare. The threat to life, health and safety would be constant. The risks and uncertainties would be onerous, and electricity made from nuclear power would be relatively high in cost as compared to thermal and hydro power. Even the OPEC caper, in its heyday, did not make nuclear power generated electricity cheap as compared to the other forms of generation. Three Mile Island and Chernobyl also sharpened the fear syndrome.

The legitimization process, the process by which nuclear energy gained a degree of popular support, or conversely of popular opprobrium, consisted not only of external environmental factors. People and organizations outside the public utility community, as well as inside, discussed the issues, argued over them and convinced or failed to convince each other. But as the issues were aired, and as government took sides in the first great energy debate, public utility industry members and investors began to *internalize* the signals and information. What was then done *at the firm level* was the reaction to external environmental forces and influences. This public and private debate over nuclear power began shortly after World War II.

Some Public Utilities (PUs) moved quickly toward nuclear investments, others less quickly, still others not at all. What each firm did, consciously or unconsciously, was to make strategy plans about the future. What would the world be like 2–5–10–15 years hence? How then should a firm meet the future? PUs are different from most industries because the former tend to be legal monopolies while the latter, generally speaking, are competitive. However in the strategic planning process of the internalization of perceived or assumed future environments, it is the organization and structure of the firm, the internalities, which are changed as well as goals. Ultimately the culture of the firm is affected. The current degree of competition is not the great issues. The nature of the future world is.

In passing, we should note that monopolies are in a better position than competitive firms to control their futures because of the lack of competition. The computer business, both hardware and software, from the 1960s to the present is an illustration of the difficulty of guessing what the competitive future will bring. IBM with its hold on the large scale mainframe industry is more secure, generally speaking, than IBM the personal computer producer. But no firm in the small computer business can afford to take it easy with respect to sales, production or product improvement. The reality of the market is too fluid.

It now appears that a sharp distinction between the environmental and the invironmental process is an illusion. They are, from the viewpoint of the firm, part of the same process. An unaffected firm is insulated against environmental force. A law regulating the quality of the air we are immersed in, if it is effective as a regulating mechanism, also regulates or at least influences the organization, structue, production technologies, output etc. of the firm. If the firm does not pollute it has no problem of internalizing an alien set of regulatory procedures. Affected firms, at the onset of regulation, are required to adopt alternative modes of behavior. As time runs its course, however, the alternative ways for the firm to act will be winnowed and sifted so that only a few tested procedures are found to be effective. Both the internalizing and the non-internalizing, i.e. unaffected firms, probably will be forced into a new set of relative price positions as a result of the change in regulation.

2 Means and Ends

A regulation by law or administrative rule, however, usually presupposes an environmental goal. Often the social techniques to achieve the goal are also presented. Clean air doesn't mean air absolutely devoid of noxious chemicals. Clean air usually means that minimal amounts of fairly well defined pollutants are acceptable. The acceptable goal is set by law or adminstration ruling pursuant to law. The means to achieve the goal may also be set. Grades of fuel to be used is one possible requirement. Scrubbers may be an alternative, an alternative strengthened by tax credits or cheap loans provided in the law or in other exact legislatively approved arrangements. Accelerated depreciation and investment tax credits immediately come to mind as legislated means for financing costly equipment..

Some economists and politicians have suggested negative means to gain the ends. Increasing taxes on polluters by making the tax rates directly proportional to the amount or changing amounts of pollution is one suggestion. Total bans on the production of certain goods, or their restricted production locations also may be a means. Zoning laws restrict the sites of manufacturing plants. Some kinds of plants simply cannot be located in some areas or neighborhoods, while the manufacture of certain goods e.g. poison gas for warfare, some insecticides, or a nuclear power installation requires government (State or Federal) license.

Such regulations may properly be considered regulations of the market. The firm is restricted and required in its behavior e.g. health and safety, quite regardless, in the first instances, of its internal arrangements. If the internal arrangements of the firm assure that the goals of policy are met, the firm may well petition for and receive a license to proceed. In such a case, no internalization of environmental restraint is necessary. All in all, firms are self organizing rather than being manipulated from the outside.[4]

This does not vitiate zoning laws. A new brewery or an abbatoir, no matter how clean and elegant, is not likely to be permitted in a residential neighborhood. If the neighborhood grows up around a brewery, it may become the object of regulation. In Copenhagen, as I recall, the center of the city has spread to envelop a brewery. By internal design without imposed environmental pressure, the brewery has retained its manufacturing function, but has also become a tourist attraction as a beer museum with free samples!

This is probably a rare case, because as a city spreads residentially or commercially to encompass a manufacturing area, the land becomes so valuable and saleable that its use shifts from manufacturing to "higher" i.e.

more remunerative uses. The conversion of a candy factory in San Francisco to a shopping center, of an old schoolhouse in Northampton, Mass. to a block of apartments and stores, of an old downtown into a tourist attraction with a magnificent musical exhibition in Charleston, S.C. (the Spoleto Festival) are only a few examples of environmental changes resulting in environmental novelties. But really these are examples of a usual course of business change, although they are spectacular.

In general, we suggest, that the government control is more likely to be socially acceptable if it is direct rather than indirect. To allow water pollution, upon the payment of a fee, even a steep fee, is offensive to the moral sense of many people. If polluting water is wrong, then stop it. To allow the erring firm to "buy off" government by a payment, even a payment higher than the cost of cleaning the water, seems underhanded, even immoral. To help the firm devise a way to stop the pollution is, on the other hand, more likely to have social acceptance. Ideas of control by countervailing costs probably makes little political sense to the electorate.

As interest rates fluctuate, as wages rise, or as technology improves, firms adjust their behavior, structure, organization and their plans to meet or fit what the managers consider the new realities. All do not react and act the same way. Regulation always has the risk that, after regulations are issued firms will simply pay no attention to them. The problems of enforcing government regulations are myriad. Effective responsibility implies the ability to put into effect a program to enforce the regulations. Government frequently lacks the will and/or ability to carry out the tasks.

Of course not all, nor even most internal changes are due to government regulation. Perceptions of the market and expectations lead firms to expand, contract, merge, change their product, or do whatever managers see fit to do, under the law.

Our point is fairly obvious, but, in its open visibility, often overlooked. The environment, no matter how constructed, affects firms by requiring the invironment to change and adjust. Nor can one foretell with complete accuracy, often with even tolerable accuracy, what internal changes will be forced upon a firm as a result of environmental influences. Such planned actions of a firm are a large part of what has come to be known as Strategie Planning (S.P.). That is to say a firm tries to estimate (a) what is the likely shape of the future (10 years hence, for example) with respect to demography, technology, taxes, regulations, new products, etc. and (b) its possible place in a market, its market share, in the light of future changes in the markets it will service.

3 Planning of Means and Ends

A strategic plan, with contingency opportunities for changed direction by the firm and market, is then constructed not as a map or blue print, but as a suggested set of goals, means, obstacles and undertakings. In a sense the firm tries to project a relevant picture of the future as history and considers how to operate in such circumstances. The (b) part is the parochial part, and always subject to revision by the (a) part. But (a), too, is subject to review and recasting. Sociological, political, economic and econometric models become the products of (a) and (b).[5]

Rarely, if ever, are the micro or parochial and the macro or universal guesses going to be correct. The question is: "Does strategic planning provide a better insight and suggest better models of the future than other brainstorming techniques?" Our biased guess is that S.P. does, and is always a necessary, undertaking of management. The firm's leaders may not use formal, technical measures and modes, but since every action has the implication of futurity in it, everyone who undertakes an action must have some implicit or explicit hypothesis about the future.

The easiest one is that the future will be like the present and like the past. Experience casts great doubt on the validity of that kind of philosophy of history. Currently, computer devised models are fairly easy to come by. But computer models, i.e. "guestimates" about future market shares and relations, or technological changes, or even political developments are only as good as the wisdom and luck of the model builder. Statistically, mechanically minded program inventors, however, are not particularly nor uniquely gifted as social philosophers and "futurists", to use a word which had a brief popularity. The timing and technology associated with actions in the future are not always well handled elements in model building. But these two depend on many considerations which give shape and substance to the forecasted future. So S.P. is a necessary, ever present, but difficult exercise because it is an attempt to make the forecast compare with the future reality.

The micro means and ends of social action are generally dedicated to requiring some action of people and firms (institutions). These are often specific law, rules and actions. The macro actions–the actual results and means of general policy–are not always those which the society expected or wanted. Incidentally it is not impossible that in rare cases the expectations of S.P. actually affect the new state of affairs. Guesses by big firms or governments may be realized because of the social authority of the makers of the guesses.

Our point is the particular micro effects must be *particularly* viewed, and the macro effects, too, are *particularly* significant. However, the word particular, in the first instance, is a micro modifier, in the second, a macro adjective. But each is particular in that the outcome of the act can only be appraised by specific evaluation.

In regulation the goals are generally more significant than the means. Means, however, may be seen as ends if the business horizon extends but briefly into the future. A six month or year result of a policy need not be the same as the 5 or 10 year result. What appears as a goal of legislation and policy may also well be a means to another end. For example, public education is often seen as an end in itself. And indeed the educational process, in itself, may be an enjoyable experience. But educated people are also more civil, and civilized, more economically productive, make better citizens, and so on, than the less educated. Therefore, education is a process, a means as well as an end of society. Indeed since education can be acquired in a number of ways, and has a number of results, it is both a process of multiple means and multiple ends. The changing nature of means and ends is an inherent part of the social process.

Government decrees clean water or clean air, for example. This is a social goal. The firm's managers decide that the firm shall do this and that, within certain parameters of water or air cleanliness. The decrees of the firm's managers may be in two areas: (1) mechanics (2) values or ideology. The firm may buy a piece of scrubbing or purifying equipment or change its coal or raw material sources. These are physical, even structural changes. But the managers may also decree that better records will be kept to measure the impurity of air and water as a result of the manufacturing process to secure proper levels of air and water purity. Record keeping is an important prelude to behavior change, but so is the information flow from inside and outside the firm to responsible technicians and managers or to government. Sales policy, buying policy, plant upkeep and tidiness, cost and returns data, and other informational gambits may be enhanced and used to control operations. These are cultural manifestations, eventually becoming environmental and invironmental.

From the macro viewpoint of evaluation of the success or failure of a regulatory program and policy, as well as from the micro measures of the firm, money measures alone are not very convincing. The firm, of course, to remain in the market as a viable member of the industry, must show a reasonable profit, satisfactory share of market, and promise of staying in business. We are referring to the usual market measures of success and failure of a firm. But the macro measure, the environmental regulation which give rise to the exercise, cannot easily, some would say possibly, be reduced to money costs and returns alone. The will of managers to perform in accordance with non money values is significant.[6]

Cost/benefit analysis to determine how best to perform a business task is, at best, a makeshift. First, as the textbooks tell us, the units of cost we customarily deal with are monetary while the benefits may be, in appreciable part, social or personal i.e. not easily nor satisfactorily given a money value. The cost of building a public park is an accounting and/or economic measure of dollars and opportunity. The use value of the park is harder to estimate. Beauty, relaxation, and other psychological benefits and costs are not reducible to money measures. But the *opportunity costs* of economics are also not easily measured in dollars. Clear water and clean air are undoubtedly possible to achieve if business, government and consumers want a clean environment seriously enough to pay for it. The costs are not only in money but in the willingness to accept social change which may be costly in goods produced or not produced, employment practices, taxes, in short, on limitations on freedom. The benefits as well as costs, however figured, are distributed over many people and a long period of time. Interpersonal and, we may add, intertemporal utilities and disutilities, are usually considered not to be comparable.

In point of fact, however, in ordinary living we constantly make interpersonal and intertemporal comparisons. Every time a tax is levied it affects different people differently, even if they enjoy comparable money incomes. The millionaire with 4 children at home, even after the piddling allowances for personal exemptions, pays a different sum of utilities (in the form of taxes) than the millionaire with no children to feed and educate. Similarly the benefits paid to unemployed workers have different personal utilities depending on local cost of living, weather and climate, personal experiences, attitudinal differences and so on. Saving now for income later represents an intertemporal evaluation. Social status, social expectations, and self perceptions all play roles in integrating interpersonal and intertemporal utility considerations. Currently, the social differences between Japanese and the American ideal types of saving and spending have generated a great discussion of the role of Japan in the world economy, just as the role of U.S. production and consumption habits have generated discussion and debate in the past..

4 Means and Ends as Conjectures

Yet in spite of all these and other known dissimilarities among people who are payers or receivers of costs and benefits, we constantly compare costs and benefits and interpersonal utilities. We, as a society, as parents, as public officials, as anyone with responsibility, make such comparisons because they are necessary to keep the world together as an operating entity. Solipsism may have nothing wrong with it as a philosophical concept, as philosopher Bertrand Russell is reported as having said, but in practice and in our illusions of reality, (to give solipsism a break) we live in a world of interacting people. As dynamic knowledge and experience push against the *status quo* of ignorance, we have new perceptions and conceptions of reality. Regularly and without much excitement all of us do the impossible, we compare incomparables.[7]

5 Heterogenity as a Norm

Institutions are, by our definition, social modes of behavior. Each member of an institution rarely if ever totally conforms to all the prescriptions and value systems of that institution. All Catholics are not clones of the Pope nor of the local Bishop. Nor do all Republicans think the same on every issue. Capitalism, too, has a variety of faces. But Catholics, Capitalists, Republicans or for that matter Democrats and Economists, anyone who, by choice or chance accepts a general social view which has been crystallized into a more or less formal social habit, does share *some* values, ideals and moralities with his fellows in the institution. Thus adherence to a political party is a belief in a general way of thinking, evaluating, and acting, which many people share. They tend to vote for the Party and believe, more or less, in its tenets. They tend to support the Party by deeds and funds. Such people, to the degree of their Party loyalty, find a moral legitimation in the Party, thus justifying their loyalty and obedience.

The dynamics of a political Party are not unlike the dynamics of preparing a dinner. The small parts and tasks must more or less fit together ideologically (or aesthetically). They must also fit together in time, so that simultaneity between and among parts is attained when judged appropriate, and seriality is attained when it is deemed appropriate. Just as the soup may not follow the dessert at dinner, so the pressing an issue before its time can be disastrous.

What the cook of our dinner, the party leader, and the planners in any institution require, *inter alia* as a necessary mode of behavior is what management observers call contingency planning. That is to say, ways to shunt problems aside, to create new hierarchies of importance, to change the direction of what is being done, to provide alternate means and ends to an ongoing course of behavior, must be found or better *built into* the planning process.

All planners must, if they are to be successful, be ready to adjust their behavior and goals. Otherwise they and their plans will be, at some time, rejected in a real world where the requirements for institutional persistence are fluidity and adaptation.

So the party leaders cannot come to the electorate too late or too early. What is too late or too early is a determination which is part of the art of political leadership, rather than a clock time decision. The party leaders, politicians and observers of the political scene, like business people and observers of business and markets, take it for granted that political and administrative decisions, including legal decisions, have an influence on markets and business behavior and organization.

The essential legitimating ideas of the institutions of business, law and policies are similar to the point of being identical. Our remarks, it should be noted, apply to a democratic society such as the U.S. in which ideas of liberty, freedom and individualism on the one hand, and equality for individuals on the other, are at the core of the legitimations of the political, legal and economic social structures.[8]

6 The Modern Spirit

By and large the Western World's social legitimation seems to include the following propositions:

1 Self interest is a powerful motivating force in social and private action. Self interest does not, in general, end up as being self serving, for what starts out to be a selfish act, due to competition, becomes a benign conglomeration of social ends. This is the social defense of private competition.

2 Self interest requires individual freedom and liberty to act, always restricting self interest actions from restricting, in an inappropriate way, someone else's liberty and freedom to act in his/her self interest. This implies a moral or governmental restraint. (1 and 2 thus might give rise to conflicts in policy).

3 The State is a necessary regulatory agency to protect competition and restrain monopoly. (Government therefore exists and is based on some sort of social contract, i.e. is legitimated by the contract.) The regulations and undertakings of the State should be limited to assuring some acceptable idea of justice and fairness, and to performing services for society which it can do more cheaply and effectively than can a private, self interest motivated institution. Examples of appropriate social action are national defense, internal security, water supplies, and street cleaning. The State responds to public pressure but is the responsible keeper of the basic ideals e.g. the Court System.

4 Protection (sanctity?) of contract and of private property rights are among the duties of government, for without them self interest cannot be effective. (3 and 4 might be in conflict for justice and fairness may apply to individuals as people as well as to groups). How does a State or anyone else, compare the welfare of persons vs the welfare of people? Are there universal critieria of measurement, or is judgment i.e. no preagreement on criteria indicated? This conundrum also applies to contract and private property as "rights". Are the obligations connected with rights always known and agreed on before an issue arises, or is the society so dynamic that judges and law makers cannot quite define rights until *after* an issue arises or the question posed?

5 Efficiency is a good attribute of economic undertakings. Efficiency leads to more goods at cheaper prices and more is better than less, and cheaper better even than cheap. Short and long run considerations are involved but are not always in accord. Free international trade may benefit consumers in the long run, but, in the short run, *some* consumers and producers may suffer due to loss of income and loss of jobs. Economic adjustments take time and are beset by frictions.

6 Amenity is the imposition of rules of work or other market conditions by such social means as legislative actions, public opinion or administrative ruling. Amenity is designed to ease the burden of earning a living, or just living for those who need help in this precarious world. Need

is defined in the rule or legislation, but less well defined in public opinion. Examples are hours of work rules, safety and health rules, contract rules, and pure food and drug rules. (5 and 6 may obviously be in conflict.) This conflict is the basis of the differences between the so called Chicago Legal School or conservative view of regulation and what we might call the critical realist, constitutional view. Chicago, generally holds that in a world of economic scarcity, efficiency should as a matter of policy, be encouraged and not restrained. The other view is that efficiency in the market can be devastating to some. Neither justice nor fairness are always assured by the free, competitive market, therefore social legislation is legitimated. The question of *how much* efficiency and *how much* amenity and of what kinds are, of course, vital issues. There is no absolute answer, there are only social judgments which from time to time command differing majorities and arguments. It is not an "either or" problem for either liberals or conservatives. It is a particularistic kind of problem.

7 Freedom, liberty, individualism, all are more or less synonyms for each other as we are using the words. They are logically prior to self interest. One must be able to act, free to perform before he/she can act purposively. Government is the means of assuring liberty. Government is a means, a tool, not an end. Markets, too, are modalities and not ideals. Like all means, government and market are not so efficient as one should like. So government and markets have to be carefully watched lest they become tyrants in the guise of regulators. Ideologies with uncritical affection for government and/or markets may become a source of injustice, unfairness and ethics.

8 Equality is essential in a free society. What is meant by equality gives rise to confusing points of view. Equality is perhaps a misnomer. A more expressive set of words might be "minimally assured social means for individual persons and all people subject to a nation's jurisdiction to have the opportunities to attain socially acceptable standards of life." By persons we mean individuals, by people we mean groups, e.g., Blacks, women or defined minorities as well as all people.

The conceptual nature of the basic ideals is vast. The vastness of the ideal of social and private goodness might be stated as more or less than the 8 aspects we have listed.

The application of the essential, legitimated rights has been dramatically extended by the general extension of *equality* to the population at large. Equality, a constitutional basis for competition and thus self interest, generally has meant equality *before the law*. The American Constitution which originally explicitly assured this to white males and by implication to white women, failed to assure it to *all* persons who were citizens or merely people within the confines of federal or state coverage. That is to say women, black people, later yellow people were not covered by all the words of the Constitution. It took a Civil War and years of agitation to extend generally the concept of equality *before the law*. Even now the unborn are being represented in law and politics by persons unrelated to the unborn. They argue for the constitutional rights of the fetus.

As the American and Western Societies developed socially, economically, and politically the idea of equality before the law was not enough to satisfy the craving for personal independence. The idea that in order to be equal, people had to be *assured* some level of opportunity for education and income became fairly commonplace. Equality before the law is a fairly obvious right. But equality implies the need for the franchise, education, income and opportunities. Such means to a decent life require more than equality before the law. This is what the whole exercise of a free society is about.[9]

So equality was extended to include assurances that the means (the vote, education, income transfers and equal opportunity) would be guaranteed by government. The guarantees are minimal – food and shelter above a poverty level, equality of minimal free education for all eligible, absolute assurance of the franchise and a fair trial, the right to work as a civil right, and under, as yet undefined conditions, possibly the right to life of the unborn.

Such extensions of equality are neither generally accepted as specific rules nor totally understood in their implications. Needless to say, 6, 7 and 8 contain major issues of policy and ideology which presently internally divide the American and other societies. The issues create long or short lived coalitions of interest groups, and in general, make the present age so exciting. An exciting age is easier to live through in retrospect than on a day to day basis. Actually living in an interesting, exciting age is a painful task, at best.

The moral issues and the technical means to win the goals finally agreed on create social conflict, divisiveness and enormous drains on knowledge and social inventiveness. Such demands are not the bases for a harmonious, ideologically secure society, but may be the basis for a progressive society.

This conception implies, *inter alia,* income transfers and power transfers which automatically impinge on the freedom of those who are taxed for these purposes or placed in a less favored economic or social position. To assure the vote to minorities inevitably reduces the power of the old majority. To create the opportunities and legitimations in business or politics for new coalitions reduces the power of the old coalitions. Power is at the heart of the New Equality. Where the New Equality will lead the society no one really knows. What seems clear is that the idea that equality and freedom are each good i.e. ethical in its own right although different, and that each should be widely spread.

The factors and forces which we consider essential to democratic social life are:

1 Self interest – as a concept, with potentially damaging perceptions.
2 Freedom and liberty – as a concept, with varying perceptions.
3 The State (as responsive and responsible).
4 Contract and Private Property Rights.
5 Market Efficiency.
6 Market Amenity.
7 Freedom as a dynamic.
8 Equality as a dynamic.

They are what hold the society together, largely through the traditions, constitutions, and the judgement of those appointed to judge i.e. the judiciary administrators, managers, and finally the molders of Public Opinion. Those are the great legitimators. Their ideals or drives also expose to the Society the great, divisive social issues which are based on the allocation and use of power. Social change and reform tends to derive from the interconnections of the 8 forces.[10] Ideology, hence public and private ethics are embedded in all the concepts.

Clean air and water, nuclear waste, social and labor legislation, the regulation of student loans, concern over the poor and the homeless, education, abortion, drugs, price levels, employment, social harmony, production, progess, all these and ultimately more are issues whose solution or non-solution ultimately rests on the 8 basic ideas, we dare say. They are among the Constitutional perceptions which play so great a role in American national history and indeed in the history of the Western World.

To be sure the basic conceptions of the 8 may be enumerated as more or fewer ideas and ideals. What we are trying to do is suggest the ultimate structural nature of a society commonly viewed as "Democratic Capitalism." In Europe such a society tends to be also designated "Democratic Socialism." We see the structural nature as a social jurisprudence, and for economic life a jurisprudence of markets and business.

7 Ideals

As essential as the social drives are, their own legitimization, in American and many other societies rests on additional basic, Utopian ideas, which in their turn are dynamic and all inclusive. They are Justice, Fairness, and Ethics.

Justice, in our view, is an idea of reward and punishment for individual undertakings. A person who gets what he/she deserves gets justice. This tautological statement is not far afield from the economic theoretical point of the marginal productivity theory of income distribution. By this, each factor of production receives a share of income equal to the factor's contribution to the production process. The marginal product of F(actor) times the number of F(actoral) units = the reward of Factor F. In an integrated, complex production system the marginal product is, at best, a guess or tautology. Whatever a factor gets is its contribution. In a non-theoretical construct, the marginal product is an idea and ideal or even a metaphor. Most theory probably is metaphor about reality. This view would bring the truth of social theory closer to poetry than to an absolute or theme in itself.

Fairness is another matter. What is fair should make sense as a matter not corresponding to justice or marginal productivity, but in the light of behavior, intent and circumstance. A person who tries hard and fails can be distinguished from a person who sloughs off and horses around. The former is entitled, most would say, to more consideration (read reward) than the uncommitted performer. The committed is often entitled to another chance, or perhaps some minimal recompense for effort.

Fairness softens justice while justice protects against the soft headedness of human sympathy. Both are necessary and both are interactive in their effects. Each society, each time and place, has somewhat differing measures of justice and fairness, but all societies have some ideas of these basic principles which overlap. Justice and fairness are social. There is the doer, the actor who is being judged, and the observer, the employer as judge or team captain, and finally Society, and, in effect the courts as appeal bodies.

If justice is giving one his/her due, and fairness is an entitlement, a just payment and a proper payment for the outcome of a productive exercise, may result in a paradox. We assert this on the basis that different contributors have differing utility functions, differing values as to money income or any other income, and different commitments. Therefore equal pay for equal work does not necessarily make the personal value of a similar reward equal for persons who make identical contributions to a product exercise. To a degree the awards determined by fairness tend to even out the reward structure, fairness is an award according to the "fitness of things". But the fitness is a conventional or even highly personal perception. It tries to equalize the utilities of those who are the beneficiaries of fairness with those who are not.

Justice and fairness are not absolutes. But they are attempts to reach a level of morality which satisfies, insofar as one or a society knows the essential values of the society. The attempts to control the workings of fairness and justice is responsibility. In other words, the management and administration of the entire system of welfare distribution is the task of responsibility. Government is ultimately the responsible agency in Society.

Ethics is, in our view, a different matter. The recipient of a benefit which is bestowed by a donor, with no consideration or recompense, or only a minor recompense is the object of the ethical act. *The donor is under no social obligation to do good.* If he/she were, the matter would fall under justice or fairness. The ethical act is *sui generis*. It is not an act *required* by law or custom. Its legitimation may be social, but its reward to the donor is not a *quid pro quo*.

8 The Private and the Social Ethic

The individual nature of the ethical act has been somewhat obfuscated by the use of the words "social ethic". If a person is required to act in accord with the socially legitimated values, in short, in accord, with law, custom, convention or rule, the action may be totally desirable from a social viewpoint. But it is not ethical in the personal sense. Social ethic constrains, requires, and expects certain personal actions. A benefit, at least negatively stated as avoidance of a disbenefit, ensues for the actor. He/she is rewarded by being considered good (as the private ethical donor may be). But doing the social good either keeps one out of trouble with the law or follows the dictates of public opinion rather than being "inner directed". A private action which improves the social welfare is an ethical act. It however, is not part of the social ethic if it, in truth, is freely willed and not self serving. A law which undertook to raise the standards of education for the poor by income transfers, would, in our language, be a representation of the social ethic. In other words the social part of the social ethic is socially required as well as socially beneficial.[11]

Ideally "inner direction" requires little or no public legitimation. Usually some action is implied in the ethical act legitimation. If General Electric or Texaco undertake a selfless act, shareholders, Milton Friedman and the Internal Revenue Service may properly ask: "Who really paid for it?" The selfless act is suspect as selfish. What did GE or Texaco get out of the ideal? Was it worth it? The selfless act becomes an instrumental one very quickly if the managers try to show that the benefactor companies they manage gained more than the cost. Let a Getty give the public an art museum and a grand collection, or the Ford family donate a Ford Foundation, and skeptics raise the same question. "What was in it for them?"

And the answer is often instrumental not ethical. Things are not always what they seem. However, if someone acts as if his action were selfless, it may be worthwhile not to evaluate the actions with too much cynicism. Human motivations and behavior are rarely utterly pure or singly guided. Ethical acts in combination with instrumental overtones are not unknown. Even in the prosaic market doing good and doing well are not mutually exclusive. Ethical acts do exist. Individuals and families do set up public spirited foundations to do good, individuals do help each other, even without knowing the particular beneficiaries. As one goes through life one of the amazing and charming aspects of society and individuals is how kind, considerate and helpful people can be. It is offset, of course, by the opposite observation that people, as individuals and as groups can also be indifferent and unkind.

Justice, fairness, and ethics often occur simultaneously or, better put, are often implicit in social actions. The coalescence of the three in actions of society and individuals, is the idea of responsibility. Like ethics, it should be thoughtful and informed as well as legitimated. Unlike justice, responsibility is self and socially conscious. Unlike fairness, responsibility recognizes that social actions entail costs as well as returns.

In the light of the above, we have a useful way to look at the environment of markets and business and make some evaluations. The environment, to be sure, does not consist only of manmade, socially contrived restraints and constrains of our markets and business. There are natural forces in the environment. It is not a case of a house of many mansions in which this man is told to come and cometh and that man is told to go and goeth, with Government as the stage manager.

In general we may divide the regulatory process of markets, hence business, into two general, if overlapping categories.

A – Direct regulation
B – Indirect regulation

Direct regulation, generally speaking, consists of market regulation. Not to be allowed by law to pay less than a minimum for labor, supposedly cuts off the parts of the demand for labor of less than the minimum. The truncated demand function, by itself does not affect the supply curve directly. The restriction on demand may result in some unemployment. In subsequent periods the effect of the new unemployment may cause some members of the labor force to reconsider their options, e.g. relief vs a job or giving up looking for work (discouraged worker hypothesis), or going back to school. Thus in a simple example the possible connections between wage regulation, unemployment, reliance on various government income transfers and discouraged workers are exposed. What actually happens, of course, depends upon the particular economic and social situation. Whether government does nothing, little, or a great deal it still is part of the market environment.

Once government intervenes directly or indirectly, the repercussions may be intricate and important, and may require or suggest government actions in areas not originally contemplated. Education, money, training, income transfer, insurance policies and changes may all be affected or required as the result of what appeared to be a modest intervention. Good faith commitments, taking the regulations into account, may, from the fairness point of view, make the deregulation process difficult.

This observation is not to be construed as for or against any particular government action. It is to observe that markets house gears within gears, and myriads of relationships based on economic and psychological connections. The psychological interconnections are particularly difficult to estimate in advance because of varying expectations based on the state of the economy. The short and long run prognostications, and the tone and the temper of the times, rarely fit any narrow conceptional scheme. In retrospect minimum wages, aid to families with dependent children, unemployment insurance, training programs and so on, are all related not only to each other, but to seemingly unrelated public actions. Regulations may be considered just and fair, as well as efficient and agreeable or costly. What is planned and done affects the freedom and equality of the society as a whole as well as of particular classes of people or persons. The *intent* of government regulation, of course, may be quite different from the *results* of regulation. Motive and success are quite different categories.

9 The Complexity of Interests

So far as we can see there is no single analytical system, or application, which purports to or can resolve issues as these. As we have urged, different times generate different values. And the ongoingness of a regulatory action itself is generated by, and in turn, may generate values different from the past. Reforms often purport to improve the whole of society or humankind. But absolutes in the social setting are rare indeed. Regulations to assist one limited group or restrain another are not always well received in public opion. To be sure the greater good is generally valued as higher than a lesser good. However, hard headed, Pecksniffian arguments of costs and returns have their place. So have "goodness, truth, and beauty".

Our point is that markets, as structures, consist of many interrelated parts, so that an intervention by government may well require, even imply, additional interventions, which cannot always, perhaps usually, be done or even thought of in advance. Furthermore, the interventions themselves require legitimation as to means and ends in the light of a value system which itself is multidimensional and not constant.

Our conclusion is not that intervention by government into markets is an unalloyed mistake or immorality. Rather we conclude that because of the complexity of the problem, intervention by government should be thoughtfully considered, with a contingent backdoor of withdrawal always available. Caution and reflection are not bad ingredients in action if intent and desired result are to both be achieved.

How the power is exercised is almost as significant as the assumption of power. Both must be judged in the light of the right or power of the State to restrict freedom in the use of property. This is no small matter but, as a general rule, the sovereignty of the State justifies, under various conditions, restrictions on freedom. Capricious assumptions of private power, i.e. property and property rights by the State, are clearly improper in current democratic ideology. Regulations tend to be costly to the firms as well as to the government. If they were not, there is a good chance the government regulation would not have been needed. Benefits may be spread among the general society and its individuated segments, and among individuals. Nor are the benefits easily measured in dollars. Clean air or water, affirmative actions or changes in interest rates, each may cost the offending parties or those directly adversely affected, sums of money which can be fairly accurately measured. The social benefits, however are not easily calculated. And there may be additional social costs related to the cost of enforcement, which is in part a dollar figure, and also a cost in the wear and tear on government authority and prestige. This is a non-dollar amount.

Just as the direct interventions into the market change the ways of doing business by transforming market structure, so do the indirect interventions transform market and income structures. The redistribution of market power among the actors in the serveral markets is an important force in causing structural market change. Income transfers e.g. Social Security, training and education programs, tax exemptions and credits, public amenities in effect change the effective distribution of disposable income and of government tax receipts.

10 The Logic of Policy

What is apparent from the above few paragraphs is that political and social action for change and reform do not necessarily follow neat, logical rules nor require deep empirical underpinnings. Both logic and observation help make an argument, but ultimately ideology, belief and value, sanction it. The world is not usually grasped as a *gestalt,* as a unity, by the mass of people, including the policy makers. The world is usually grasped as a particular or a few particulars.[12]

Folk wisdom and political practice seem to require a world of second, third or n*th* best rather than a world of ideal maximization. What seems basic and overriding in reflection and analysis is what we so often tend to observe is more or less obsure, enigmatic and even poetic in action. Amenity, efficiency liberty, ideological beliefs are general ideas which lead to particularlism in action. We live in a world of particularity and think in a world of insubstantiality.

Thus policy is a sometime thing. Repeal, amendment, a new twist are or should always be possible. Old reforms which have stood the test of time, have often forced the market, regulated or unregulated, to conform not precisely to efficiency or amenity, or to freedom or equality but to the old reforms. While administrative efficiency and economy are always desireable, they pale in significance when compared to purpose, intent and the means designed to accomplish the purposes of a regulation.

The dangers, ideologically or structurally, of messing around with old reforms is enormous. It took a New Deal revolution to expand the concept of equality from only equality before the law to some minimal levels of power and income.[13]

Regulation implies decisions and decisions imply judgement. Judgement is a necessary ingredient of planful action.[14] And regulations of the future may be the subjects of control are not even guessed from the vantage of the present. Guessing what they might be is a nice task for the Strategic Social Planner.

Footnotes

[1] A. Solomon, "Economics, Ideology and Public Policy," *Challenge,* July–August, 1986, p. 11ff. Mr Solomon expertly examines the connections among ideology particular events and economic policy during 1980s.

[2] B. A. Ackerman, "Social Justice in the Liberal State," *Yale,* 1980, see p. 99ff.

[3] T. Veblen, "Why is Economics not an Evolutionary Science?" *Place of Science in Modern Civilization.* This article, written in 1898 examines the differences between a tendency and a particular circumstance. Presumably and "evolutionary" science must combine the two considerations into a developing unity.

[4] R. Marris and D. C. Mueller, "The Confirmation, Completion and The Invisible Hand," *J. of Ec. Literature,* Vol. XVIII, March, 1980, pp. 32–63.

[5] S. C. Sufrin and G. S. Odiorne, "The Strategic Planning Boom," *Rivista Internzionale c/i Scienze Economiche e Commerciali,* XXX, February, 1983, N. 2, p. 105ff.

[6] V. A. Thompson, "Modern Organization," *Knopf,* N. Y., 1961. Thompson's argument, like many organizational writers is that the modern firm puts many stresses and pressures on its members. However, the many ends are gained generally along with commitment to the institution.

[7] A. Sen, "Review of Arrow's Social Choice and Justice," *J. of Ec. Literature,* December, 1985, Vol. XXIII, No. 4, pp. 1697–1727.

[8] J. Rawls, "Distribution Shares," *A Theory of Justice,* Harvard, 1971, Chapter V, p. 258ff.

[9] Rawls ibid p. 301ff.

[10] T. Parsons, E. Shils, K. D. Naegele and J. R. Pitts (Eds), "Symbols Processes and Cultural Heritage," *Theories of Society,* Free Press, 1961, Vol. II, p. 997ff. Talcott Parsons' writing the foreword of this section asserts the interdependence of communication, signs, symbols and culture patterns. The basics of American social life contain such signs and symbols and culture patterns which are the basis or the social legitimation of private and public actions. It is

as if the ultimate legitimation is in a value *system* rather than in a part of one as self interest, or a concern with one's fellows.

[11] P. T. Heyne, "Ethical Codes: A Blind Alley," *Private Keepers of the Public Interest,* Vol. V, p. 41ff. Heyne sees ethics as what the ethical man decides it is.

[12] J. M. Clark, "Control and Economic Law," and "Can Democratic Law Succeed?" *The Social Control of Business,* Chapter XXIX & XXX, McGraw Hill, 1939, p. 473ff. Clark's contribution to the literature of business environment is, in our opinion, much greater than is generally recognized.

[13] Clark – Ibid, "Legal Framework of Economic Life," *Chapter V,* "Some Fundamental Legal Institutions," *Chapter VI,* "Law and Economic Life: Some General Problems," *Chapter VII,* p. 71ff.

[14] R. Dworkin, *Taking Rights Seriously,* "Constitutional Cases," Chapter 5, p. 131ff. Dworkin appears to relate judicial activism to popular activism. This point of view seems reasonable and gives weight to social coalitions as having a constitutional role and a novel impact.

Suggested Readings

Democracy and Leadership – Irving Babbitt, Houghton Mifflin Co. 1952
"The gap between what men do and what they ought to do is turning out to be even wider under the humanitarian dispensation than under that of medieval Christianity" (p. 314)

Montaigne's Essays – W. Z. Hazlett (ed) Vol. 3 – Chapter I – "Of Profit and Honesty" George Bell and Sons 192 2nd Edition.
"A man but ill proves the honour and beauty of an action by its utility: and very erroneously concludes that every one is obliged to it, and that it becomes everyone to do it, if it be of utility." (p. 18)

Social Control of Business J. M. Clark, McGraw Hill 1939 – 2nd Edition
"Service and efficiency are coordinate parts of any attempt to control prices, first, because it does the buyer no good to pay a lower price if the quality or quantity he gets for his money is lowered in the same proportion... Second, it does the buyer no good to compel the producer to accept half the former net earnings if he gets in exchange a management half as efficient, for the poor management will add more to the costs of operation than the regulating commission can take away in reduced earnings" p. 337

Philosophy in the Twentieth Century "G.E. Moore", – A.J. Ayer, Random House 1982.
"The principal theses of (Moore's) *Principia Ethica* are that the primary business of ethics is to enquire into the extensions of the properties 'good' and 'bad,' that good is a simple unanalysable, non natural quality; that philosophers who have identified good with pleasure, or progress in evolution or any other natural property, have committed what Moore calls 'the naturalistic fallacy', that a similar fallacy has been committed by those philosophers who have identified good with some metaphysical entity ... that egoism is irrational ... that right action is, by definition, the one ... that would have the best effects; that since the effects extend indefinitely into the future we never know what actions are right, there is however, a probability that we act rightly when we follow generally accepted rules ...' p. 41–42.

Fairness and Justice – C. M. Haar and D. W. Fessler, Simon and Schuster 1986.
"...the words of the courts are the still relevant harvest of centuries of social, political and legal change." (p. 8)

Ethics and Public Policy – Tom L. Beauchamp and Terry P. Pinkard (eds) – Prentice Hall 1983.
"The issue here is: Where should we draw the line between conduct that is required and conduct that is good although no required, so as to get the best possible result?" (Peter Singer in Beauchamp and Pinkard) (p. 198)

Right and Wrong – Christina Hoff Sommers (ed), Harcomt Brace Jovanovich 1986.
"If you wonder about the reasons behind the ugly mixture of cynism and guilt in which most men spend their lives, these are the reasons: cynicism because they neither practice nor accept the altruism morality – guilt because they dare not reject it." (p. 178) (Ayn Rand in Sommers)

Ethical Theory and Business – Tom L. Beauchamp and Norman E. Bowie, Prentice hall 1979.
"First: each person is to have an equal right to the most extensive basic liberty compatible with a similar liberty for others."
"Second: social and economic inequalities are to be arranged so that they are both (a) reasonably expected to be to everyone's advantage, and (b) attached to positions and offices open to all - - - [The Difference Principle] John Rawls in Beauchamp and Bowie (p. 39)

Ethics and the Executive – Clarence C. Walton, Prentice Hall 1969.
"Every executive - - - seeks an "action guide" which can reconcile individual needs with societal needs; the "action guide" includes personal norms and social values, and the objective is to achieve a workable harmony between the two - - (T)he effort is to assure that technical decisions are informed by value principles and infused by concern for human and humane goals" (p. IX)

Business Ethics – Richard T. De George – Macmillan 1982.
"... (M)oral judgments are judgments which can and should be defended but for which better or poorer arguments are often given. If we are faced with contradictory judgments about an action, only one of them can be right" (p. 34)

Management of Business Ethics Sidney C. Sufrin Kennikat Press 1980.
"Ethics deals with the distribution of power and wealth as part of its concern" (p. 75)

Index

Adams family 18
administrative incursions 17
administrative rule 155
amenity 46, 51, 97, 120, 127
American evangelical fundamentalsim 27
animal spirits 22
Anti Trust 18
associations of people 23
authority 97

Bauhaus 78
beauty 78
Bentham 56
Bernard Shaw, George 11
Blough, Roger 54
Brown Shoe Co 20
Buckley 32
Buckley, William 31
Burger 140
business policy 98

Catholic Bishops 27
CIA 22
Clark, J.M. 32
Common Law 27
communal organizations 23
comparable work 39
computer devised models 157
conservative 18, 26
conspiracy 58
constrain 119
contingency opportunities 157
contractual 99

Coolidge 18
cynicism 168

Debreu 18, 139, 140
discrimination 67
Drucker, Peter 68

efficiency 16, 46, 47, 97
efficient 127
efficient markets 102, 103
El Salvador 22
entitlement 67, 98
environment 150
equal pay 166
equal work 166
equity 32
ethical act 40
ethical actions 107
ethical obligation 99
ethics 39, 97, 98, 166
evil 116
ex market correctives 118
externalities 74

fairness 18, 38, 96, 117, 167
Falwell, Jerry 27
fitness of things 167
Ford Motor Company 55
Ford, Henry 54
France 12
France, Anatole 11
Franklin, Ben 40
free markets 100
Friedman 18
functional distribution 95

Galbraith 18, 32
Galbraith, Commons 32
Galbraith, Kenneth 31
generating inequality 32
Gilder 32
Gilder, George 31
goods 27
Graham, Billy 27
Great Depression 21
ground rules 99
guide lines 65

Hayek 18
Heilbronner, Robert 32
historical values 43
Hitler 131
Hobbes 104, 105
Hoover, Herbert 18

ideology 50, 134
income maximization 22
income transfers 47, 94
industrial bribery 27
inner direction 168
institutional constraints 134
institutions 121
instrumental overtones 168
internalizing 154
intervention 17
invironment 150

Jefferson 22
Jonesville 23
judgment 27, 39, 130
just 39
justice 18, 38, 39, 96
justice 117
justice, fairness 166

Keynes 15, 22
Keynesian liberals 18
Keynsian synthesis 152

laissez faire 121
Law of Nature 101
legitimation 130, 131
liberal 18, 26, 27
Lincoln's Proclamation 22
Locke 104, 105
Louisiana territory 22

manager 70
managerial behavior 52
marginal productivity theory of income distribution 166
market control 59
market failures 74, 117
market intervention 67
market or business ethics 45
market reorganizations 94
market system 15
markets 15
Marshall 18
material interests 61
Mondale 21
monopoly 59
moral imperialism 84
morality 134

neighborhood effects 74
Neo classical 152
New Individualism 89
Nicaraguan 22
Nozick 94, 96
nuclear power 151

Pareto 94
Pareto optimality 94
particularistic point of view 26
per se 52, 87
Pigou 18
policy makers 26
private acceptance 93
private welfares 18
production 99

177

rational expectations 102, 103
rational justification of the state 104
rationality 21
Rawls 95, 96
Reagan 18, 49
regulation 154, 155
Ricardo 18
ritual 23
rule of reason 52, 59
rules 50, 62, 119

safety net 24
Salvadoran 22
Samuelson 18
scientific management 146
Senator Hart 25
setting 14
Shaw 12
shoddy 27
Simon 140, 141
situational legitimation 130
Smith, Adam 18, 50
social ethics 18
social sanction 42
social structure 23
social value structure 40, 89
social welfare 18
socialists 18
Solow 18
status quo 132
Stevens, Justice 139, 140
Stigler 18
strategic plan 157
Strategic Planning (S.P.) 156
substantive intrusion 99
Sumner Slichter 102
Sunday, Billy 27
Supreme Court 139

technology 16
the American Constitution 164
The Establishment 43
The Good 33

Thurow, Lester 32
Tobin 18
trade off 27
trust ideology 17

U.S. Steel 55
utilitarian conception 95
utility functions 166

value free 101
Viet Nam 132

Watergate scandal 48
welfare considerations 127
welfare economics 95
whistle blowing 27, 67, 68
Wijk, Gosta 11
Women's Movement 132
working to rules 71